Becoming
Heroines

Becoming Heroines

*Unleashing Our Power
for Revolution
and Rebirth*

ELIZABETH CRONISE McLAUGHLIN

PORTFOLIO / PENGUIN

Portfolio / Penguin
An imprint of Penguin Random House LLC
penguinrandomhouse.com

Most Portfolio books are available at a discount when purchased in quantity for
sales promotions or corporate use. Special editions, which include personalized
covers, excerpts, and corporate imprints, can be created when purchased in large
quantities. For more information, please call (212) 572-2232 or e-mail specialmarkets@
penguinrandomhouse.com. Your local bookstore can also assist with discounted bulk
purchases using the Penguin Random House corporate Business-to-Business program. For
assistance in locating a participating retailer, e-mail B2B@penguinrandomhouse.com.

LIBRARY OF CONGRESS CATALOGING-IN-PUBLICATION DATA
Names: McLaughlin, Elizabeth Cronise, author.
Title: Becoming heroines : unleashing our power for revolution and rebirth/
Elizabeth Cronise McLaughlin.
Description: [New York] : Penguin / Portfolio, [2021] | Includes index.
Identifiers: LCCN 2021003304 (print) | LCCN 2021003305 (ebook) |
ISBN 9780593087671 (hardcover) | ISBN 9780593087664 (ebook)
Subjects: LCSH: Women executives. | Leadership in women.
Classification: LCC HD6054.3 .M38 2021 (print) | LCC HD6054.3 (ebook) |
DDC 658.4/092082—dc23
LC record available at https://lccn.loc.gov/2021003304
LC ebook record available at https://lccn.loc.gov/2021003305

Printed in the United States of America
1st Printing

BOOK DESIGN BY CHRIS WELCH

For Megan Baker,

who embodied it all

And for my daughter and my son,

who made me a heroine

CONTENTS

Section One

Recognition

Section Two

Reconciliation

Section Three

Revolution

Section Four

Rebirth

FOREWORD

Black women are heroines. For generations, we have fought for our survival, for our families, and for a better future. Despite the unspeakable harms and losses that have historically and routinely been perpetrated against us through to the present day, we continue to claim power, to work for justice, to seek to live in joy and to thrive. This book is an invitation for all women to do the same.

I first met Elizabeth in 2018 in Washington, DC, at Black Women's Roundtable, during a meeting in then-senator Doug Jones's office about the work that remains to be done in the Alabama Black Belt. Over the next few days, Elizabeth and I spoke about collaborating to get out the vote, leveraging and building alliances across her platform and mine, and hope for the future. Since then, we have become friends and allies in mutual support of voting rights, anti-racism work, organizing, and the broader efforts to create change.

I have watched Elizabeth walk the talk in her own leadership, work relentlessly to investigate her own biases, and center on the work of Black, brown, and Indigenous women while also mobilizing all women to create change. Her own leadership has transformed over time, and she has inspired countless women to use their voices for change.

This book is a culmination of Elizabeth's work to create a new model of leadership that redefines how we measure success based on the good we do in our own lives and in the world, that challenges white women in particular to investigate their internalized biases and to abandon the trappings of white privilege and complicity, and that walks arm in arm with all women toward collective liberation.

In my work as the cofounder of Black Voters Matter, I seek to mobilize my community, to remind all those who are struggling that they have power, and to lead with love. This book does the same. It is a profound road map for how the world can change, how whole systems of oppression can die, if we choose to do the work of understanding how those systems have harmed us and we seek to transform them from the ground up. This book speaks directly to why we, as women and across the multitude of our diversities, need to collaborate and conspire to build a better future together, because none of us are free until all of us are free.

Black women's liberation, and indeed the liberation of all people, isn't dependent on white acceptance—and can't be. The racist and misogynist systems in which we live harm all of us, and must therefore be dismantled for all of us to realize our full potential.

My hope for this book is that its readers recognize that all women have heroines within us, and that for all women to truly become heroines, we must live into leadership that demands equity and equality for all. We must conspire to dismantle hate, discrimination, and violence wherever we encounter it. We must recognize that love is the highest and most important calling, and that silence is not an option where harm remains.

In other words, we must become the heroine within, for ourselves, for our ancestors, and for future generations.

This is a spiritual quest, as well as a personal and political one, and it is not easy. The stakes, however, could not be higher. We are all linked in a collective destiny that depends on our success, and we must not stop. In the words of Ella Baker, "We who believe in freedom cannot rest until it comes."

It is a great blessing to be called to this work. May you rise to the invitation offered in this book and become the heroine the world needs right now in whatever way you can.

I look forward to meeting you on the march forward.

LaTosha Brown
cofounder of Black Voters Matter

Into the Valley of the Shadow of Death

Megan died on a Thursday night in May, two months and two days after my kids and I went into lockdown for COVID. For more than four years, she had been my right-hand person, the head of community and social media at my company, and a dear friend. Her death came suddenly—in January, she was diagnosed with cancer, and on May 14, 2020, she was gone.

Early May was a blur of percipient grief. I learned Megan was terminal in a text message from her, which revealed that after four rounds of chemo, her cancer had recurred and there were no more options. It was a matter of days until she was no longer conscious. Calls went out to all the women in our community who knew and loved her. We spent those twelve days in communication with her family in Colorado, and with one another over daily texts, phone calls, bizarrely comforting Zoom meetings, waiting for news, knowing the end was near.

In addition to being a teacher, a guide, and a brilliant strategist, Megan was also a shaman. She spent three years in her early fifties in shamanic study with a Native American teacher, and I had the benefit of witnessing Megan's talents in this regard firsthand. It was no surprise, then, when strange, out-of-this-world things began to happen as the veil between life and death opened up for Megan.

Our collective of women holding watch began to report that Megan was showing up in dreams with messages for each of us and for each other. I had an incredibly detailed dream of a visitation from her, where she described what she was setting up for me as she hovered in liminal space, that ended with the repeated message "the debt is paid." In another, she arrived to literally help me forge through a stream of rapids to get to the other side of trauma. Others in our group received messages from her about children or lovers or purpose. As we circled around one another, listening to her as she walked between worlds, these messages got stronger and stronger.

All of 2020 was strange, but this window of twelve days in May waiting for the arrival of death will long feel to me like the strangest. Every day at around 4 p.m., I would sit on my back porch here in Southern California, and begin texting Megan's sister for updates, and then move on to texting with our circle of women holding watch. I would pay attention to the earth, to the birds that appeared overhead, to the movement of the breeze and to the weather. Every day, it was like stepping through a portal into a space between here and there, with her, with all of us. She was on a bridge between worlds, and we began to walk it with her.

The day before she passed, I was sitting outside when a strong breeze came through and all of a sudden, I felt her presence. There was a whisper in my ear, and I felt her standing beside me. There's no way to describe what happened next without sounding a little in-between-worlds, but just go with me: I heard her voice.

"Bring the rain," she said. "Tell them all to do it. Show me you can do it; show me you know how. Show me you know what you need to know."

It was the oddest request. I had no idea what it would entail, but I knew what it was: it was a demand to *prove* to her that we knew what we, this circle of women, were capable of changing, that we understood our power, and that it was OK for her to go.

I put out the call to our circle. "Bring the rain," I said, and no one responded like they thought I was nuts. I waited for an impulse for what to do next.

Never one for grand gestures like controlling the weather, I walked outside onto that porch with my kids. I looked at the sky, and I said to them, "We're going to bring the rain." It was a sunny day. Neither of the kids looked at me like I was crazy. My daughter stood there with me, totally believing that we could do this, and we swept our arms to the sky, looked to the clouds in the west, toward the Pacific Ocean that was there but that we could not see, and we gestured to pull those clouds to us, right over our house, by force of will and by force of belief that we could.

Coincidence or not, something shifted. The wind began to kick up. Something moved in the air and all of a sudden the dust on the patio was swirling and the temperature dropped. Lo and behold, the clouds began to move, and things began to get, well, weird. I watched that bank of clouds move over my house. I stood there, breathing it in. I left the presence of now and realized I was well within the space of what could not be explained by rational thought. Curiously, I've never felt so simultaneously powerful and grounded, while also out of my own body, in my entire life. It was as though I had stepped into ritual and space, something ancient and modern at the same time, and found skills that were buried in my DNA that I never knew I had—skills that were needed here and now as they were needed thousands of years before, and that would serve me and the collective moving forward.

As the clouds rolled in, I put on the music that we were playing to Megan all around the world, and that her sister was playing for her at night. The song, by Sara Bareilles, is called "Saint Honesty," and the word that runs through every chorus? *Rain*. I paused. I listened. I breathed. I closed my eyes.

And a few minutes later, my daughter ran inside the house to where I stood. "Mommy!" she said. "We did it! We made it rain!" And sure enough, there on the back patio was a splattering of raindrops, just begun. We had done it, out of nothing. On a sunny day, out of nowhere, we had brought the rain.

And then, in an instant, my phone began to blow up with messages from our circle of women. Rain in Boston. Rain in New York City. Rain in Hawaii. Rain in the Midwest. Rain *everywhere*, not predicted, out of blue skies. Rain. Rain. Rain.

It was a breathtaking moment of collective action that shook the foundations of the possible in a moment of dire grief. We witnessed it. We saw it. It was real.

The following night, I woke up to thunderstorms. Again, the messages came in from all over the country—rolling thunderstorms everywhere, right around 10 p.m. Colorado time, where

Megan lay dying. We learned the next morning that at 10:05 p.m., she'd left us.

The rain and the thunder were there to welcome her home. We got to witness her magic and her power as she departed, and it was spectacular.

I look back on that moment with a deep inner knowing of what Megan wanted. She wanted the circle of women in which she traveled so intimately to know that we were ready for what was to come—that we were ready for battle, for change, with an inherent understanding of the power we already had and the power we could create. She wanted us to know that all it takes to activate it is the belief that we have it in us. She wanted us to know that we were heroines, and that we were walking with heroines, and that we were made of magic.

She wanted these things with good reason.

By the night of Megan's death, 85,581 people had died of COVID in the United States. George Floyd had only eleven days left to live. Ruth Bader Ginsburg would be gone in four months and four days.

Megan knew what it meant to be walking in the valley of the shadow of death, and she knew that we were all walking it right there with her.

◦◦

Death has a way of ripping the veil off everything, from the most personal to the most public. COVID, of course, tore it all wide open. There is no aspect of our culture and society that survives unchanged. From work to health care to education to child care to climate change to criminal justice to systemic racism to politics—everything was set on fire. We can see, finally, in the clear light of day, all the genocidal, racist cracks at the foundation of our nation that have always been there, waiting to pull the entire structure down.

So much of what we thought we could count on as Americans is now revealed to be a part of a great lie. The reliability of our institutions, the myth of American exceptionalism, the idea that we had moved beyond the crimes at the root of us (without ever truly addressing them), have rightly been revealed in all their weakness and falsity. Everywhere, finally, we see the truth, the *injustice*, of what America has always been, and it feels as though everything is on fire.

The thing about this moment that has set American mythology alight and reduced it all to ashes, however, is that ashes make for fertile ground. While we grieve what we lost or what truths we thought we knew that have turned out to be lies, we are simultaneously laying the groundwork for what could, if we claim our power, come next. Indeed, our collective mythologies of heroines reflect this—from the Phoenix rising from the ashes, to the Hindu myth of Kali, the goddess of destruction, smeared in ash and covered in blood, dancing—*dancing*—in the cremation ground.

Why, folks often ask, would she dance when she is surrounded by such misery and death? Why dance when everything is lost, burned, gone? Why smear oneself in the remains of what we thought we knew and those we loved?

We dance in grief to celebrate that we are still alive.

We put our feet on the earth, covered in ash as war paint of what we lost, because the story isn't over, because ashes transmute into the seeds of our future.

We dance because the remains of what has burned become the place from which we are reborn.

◦◦

Over the months since Megan's death, one myth of heroines has danced around me nonstop. It is the little-known story of the Daughters of Danaus, also called the Danaids. Permit me, if you will, a brief retelling. It goes like this.

Danaus was the son of a king, and had fifty daughters. His twin brother, Aegyptus, was King of Arabia, and had fifty sons. Aegyptus commanded Danaus that his daughters must marry Aegyptus's sons. Danaus, unhappy with this order, fled with his daughters, and Aegyptus followed, threatening war if Danaus didn't hand over his daughters for their nonconsensual marriage.

To avoid bloodshed, Danaus relented. But all was not as it seemed.

All fifty of Danaus's daughters were sacrificed to this battle among brothers. On their wedding night, all but one of them was raped by her new bridegroom. On instruction from their father, however, who was determined to not capitulate to his brother, those forty-nine brides murdered their rapist husbands as they slept. Danaus had his revenge.

One of the daughters did things differently, however. Hypermestra refused to follow out her father's orders to murder her husband because her husband refused to rape her on their wedding night. Danaus was livid, and brought his daughter before the courts for refusing to carry out his murderous order. The goddess Aphrodite intervened, however, and saved Hypermestra and her husband. The couple then founded a dynasty, known as the Danaid Dynasty. She got to rule, in equity, with the husband who had refused to violate her, and who she in turn had refused to murder under order from her patriarch.

But what of the other forty-nine daughters? In most retellings, the daughters were condemned to carry water in leaking vessels to a bath designed to "wash away the sins" of murdering their husbands after rape engineered at the hands of their father and uncle in a petty dispute. The vessels never filled though, nor the bath—the water always seeping out, for all eternity. In most versions of the story, the daughters were left with this Sisyphean effort to cleanse themselves of the stain of following the orders of patriarchy, with no redress and no end, forever.

I'll ask you to hold space right now, though, for a different interpretation: what if we imagine the Daughters of Danaus to be heroines in this tale? What would that look like? Pause on that for a moment.

For the valley of the shadow of death has one more tale to tell.

◖◗

Eight scant days before the 2020 election, a fire broke out in Silverado Canyon before dawn. Thanks to the historically unprecedented speed of the Santa Ana winds combined with the absence of rain for the previous nine months, what came to be known as the Silverado fire tore through seventy-two hundred acres in Southern California in the next eight hours, destroying everything in its path.

And as it ripped down the hillside of the canyon toward the Pacific Ocean, directly in between the two stood a neighborhood: mine.

Silverado Canyon has a long and storied history of mining and ruin, starting in the mid-1800s when prospectors showed up and "laid claims" to the land that the Tongva people had lived upon for centuries. Those prospector colonizers tore holes in the canyon's earth and in her mountains, plowing into the hills looking for silver and leaving perilous conditions in their wake.

While the canyon is now largely abandoned, Silverado has not forgotten the actions taken against her by men who, for more than one hundred years, sought to plunder her most valuable resources without permission and who stole the land of the Indigenous people who cared for her. She still lives in the trauma and the vengeance of it. Tunnels left from her violent excavation are still so full of water and methane gas that as recently as 2002, two men who tried to swim them suffocated to death on the noxious air.

And now, in late 2020, Silverado Canyon was aflame.

I drove out of my town with less than a half hour's notice when the evacuation order came down, with just my kids and my dogs and barely more than the clothes on our backs. We left so quickly I forgot our passports. As we turned the corner off our street to leave, the air was thick and orange and I could see smoke plumes across the main boulevard three blocks from our home.

For the next two days, holed up at a friend's house in the Inland Empire of California, I considered, not abstractly, what it would mean to lose everything. In the middle of the night, unable to sleep and curled up on a queen-sized foldout couch, I stared at my phone, scrolling for news, as the kids slept on either side of me. The fire was within a half mile of my home, jumping streets I drove on a daily basis, as firefighters tried and failed to contain her. Six months into a pandemic, surrounded by so much death and loss, on the brink of an election that was certain to determine whether American democracy would die or live to fight another day, this one more trauma felt surreal. Why here, and why now? I obsessed over the existential and practical questions, looking for answers in the blue light of my phone in the dark.

It was at that moment that I came across an update on the location of the fire. It had jumped a major intersection and was now burning at the corner of two prophetically named streets: Ritual and Ceremony.

The fire was burning at the intersection of Ritual and Ceremony. And suddenly I inhaled.

I realized that this fire was not a purge—devastating to those in its wake to be sure—but it manifested as a reclamation. The canyon was taking back what had been stolen from her, revising the land, burning off what was no longer needed along the way. She was burning it all, as fast as she could, to make way for new growth. A ritual by fire, a ceremony for her rebirth—and maybe, just maybe, for ours.

I turned it over and over in my head, no longer worried about my stuff, my journals, our photo albums, these material things that we had left behind. I returned to the *why*, the witnessing, and what it means to start over from nothing, what it would require of me and my children and our community, and also of our nation at a moment when we were days from destruction or a chance at rebirth.

I listened to my children breathe next to me in the dark.

I listened to the silence.

We were meant to be here to watch it all go up in smoke, I thought, *to watch the end of what we thought we knew and what we thought we had, to bear witness to the destruction of what we thought was permanent and untouchable. We are here to bear witness to all of it, and to process and transmute the grief into something better.*

And if that's true, continued the thought, *then we are meant to be here now as well for still more powerful reasons. We are meant to be here to birth whatever is coming next.*

And with that, I fell asleep.

Two days later, my house was still standing, as were all the other houses in my neighborhood—a few damaged, but still there, a scant two thousand feet from the nearest fire damage. The scar of the Silverado fire is still visible from the window of the room where I sit writing this, but so is the new green growth within it.

What in the end stopped the ritual of her destruction were air tankers, full of water dumped from the sky by hundreds of firefighters from all over the nation working together in a relentless procession from the air that went on for days.

What began to heal Silverado, and saved my home in the process, was a collective of human beings who came together to pour down on her exactly what she needed to create the conditions for her rebirth.

$\spadesuit$

Here's the thing about the Daughters of Danaus: they bring the rain.

They are the filters through which every ounce of life-giving water flows to hit the earth.

Rather than suffering a hell of purgatory of never being forgiven for participating in patriarchy's sins, they are heroines who revolted against forced marriage and rape, against the sins of the father-brothers who engineered a system by which they were bartered in a battle for property.

And when the revolution against all those who sought to ruin, destroy, oppress them was over? The Daughters of Danaus, now known as the Danaids, became the water bearers, the sieves for that which is life-giving, the source of a different way of being, in collective, that fertilized the seeds that lay buried deep in the earth. They became the bearers of the means for rebirth.

For if, as heroines, we were meant to be here as everything we thought we knew went up in flames, when all that we knew or believed or hoped for was lost, and where death was omnipresent— if we were meant to be here to bear witness and to be agents of change—then we are also meant to be here to bring the rain, to create and engineer the rebirth of nations and the rebirth of hope, to be the heroines in our own stories and the heroines of water, fire, earth, and air for this time and beyond, through a profound inner knowing that *this* is *why* we are here.

We are heroines already. We just don't know it yet.

We were meant to be here when it all went up in flames.

And we are meant to be here to birth what's coming next.

We are walking the cycle of the heroine's journey right now.

And it's time to bring the rain.

THE HEROINE'S JOURNEY AND THE HEROINE WITHIN

Anyone who's ever been exposed to Greek mythology is aware of the hero's journey. In brief, a man sets off on a quest, usually due to war or a woman (we're almost always to blame), and along the way he is confronted with demons, lessons, temptations, and battles within himself and with others. Eventually, he returns home the victor, to share the spoils of war with his fellow men (of which women's bodies and service are usually a part) and to live happily ever after.

Our story, the story of the heroine, is different. Why? Well, in addition to the fact that our quest is usually to benefit the collective and not just ourselves, our learning is cyclical. Over and over again, we return to the same lessons, experiences, even similar personalities in relationships, each time peeling away the layers of awareness. One routine example of this is the way in which we encounter a similar boss in one job after another, a similar personality type in the partners we choose, or a similar experience at work or in life that calls us to learn and grow. While this may sound like a broad overgeneralization, there is not a single woman I've worked with in the past decade who hasn't had the experience of similar challenges, relationships, and archetypes coming up in her story over and over again, until the lessons that she is meant to learn and the gifts she is meant to take from each person, archetype, or process are complete.

Along the way and in each passing cycle, moreover, the heroine shares her stories with her circle of friends and allies, as others do with her. These are the true gifts we bring back through each cycle of the journey. Our stories of overcoming personal, professional, and societal challenges inform our paths as individuals and in collective, and we cycle through each phase again and again to ever greater learning and knowledge.

In contrast to the hero's journey, the heroine's journey carries with it both good and bad news in its cyclical nature. In short, once the heroine is called to her journey, it never ends. This is the moment when I am here to welcome you to yours, because as a reader of this book, you have just stepped onto the path—perhaps for the first time, perhaps again.

Critically, what the cycle of the heroine's journey creates in each of us is *endurance*. And endurance is what we need on a path that demands we combat the oppressive structures that keep us "in our place," deny our achievement, and refuse us access to power.

In our current era, patriarchal and racist structures of oppression are having a profound and public field day. Our personal and professional lives are inexorably impacted by the daily struggle to survive and thrive in the face of that, even if—and perhaps especially if—we choose to try to ignore them.

What we need to succeed as heroines—indeed, what we have always needed—are profound and powerful tools to fight back against structures of oppression every day, in every way, for as long as it takes.

HOW TO USE THIS BOOK

The aim of this book is to lead each reader through the four stages of transformation on the heroine's journey, a path traced by legend and myth, carved by feminist thinkers like Clarissa Pinkola Estés and bell hooks, pioneered by generations before us that broke with establishments, power structures, and institutions that did not truly serve them, and distilled through the prism of our lives. I've filtered them through the sieve of my own experiences and those of hundreds of fellow travelers along this path.

While the cycle of the heroine's journey is without question a progressive one, you should feel free to drop in on the stage that calls to you the most. Because the heroine's journey is one that continues in an infinite spiral, you'll eventually want to cycle through each part of this book as it informs each stage of your personal quest.

And if at some point you find yourself wondering if you've failed along the way, or come to an impasse or a dead end, I'd encourage you to use that as a catalyst for introspection. All of us falter. Inevitably, we all meet profound challenges, including our own internal demons and blind spots.

Those challenges point to the work we have not yet completed. And a reminder: as I say quite a bit, perfectionism is a tool of oppression, including when it is directed inward. Be kind to yourself. There is no true failure on the path toward your own leadership save to quit the journey, to quit learning, to quit striving to live into the purpose and mission for which you came to be here, and for the betterment of all. Trust that you'll be given opportunities for more learning, for reconciliation, for excavation, and for growth, in every arena where there is still work to be done. Enjoy those possibilities, even when they're uncomfortable, and keep going.

Throughout this process, my greatest hope is that every one of you will claim your rightful role in the world as the heroine of your own journey, as a force for good, as a woman and in collective, and most importantly in furtherance of justice and freedom for all.

Together, we can heal ourselves and one another; repair the wounds of history; reconcile our roles in collective damage; and move forward to change our institutions, our governments, and our workplaces to create freedom and equity for all.

I believe within my bones that this is why we are all here, at this moment in history, heeding this collective cry for change.

> I believe that you're a part of that, or you would not be here reading this book.
> So, welcome to your journey.
> Here's to Becoming Heroines.

A WORD ON THE LENS
OF THIS BOOK

This book is a book about the excavation and embodiment of the heroic feminine energy that lives within all of us. While specifically directed at cis and trans women and non-binary folx, this book includes lessons for the heroine that lives within each of us, and its tools concern the means by which the heroine has been buried by white supremacist patriarchy, and thereby impacts all of us, regardless of gender identity.

Throughout the book, I specifically address women (cis and trans) and non-binary folx in the context of my work at the Gaia Project for Women's Leadership. However, it is my hope that this work resonates with and benefits all gender identities, and encompasses a telling of the path of the heroine that meets each reader where the heroine resides within her, him, or them.

The use of the terms "woman" or "women" is intended herein to include all those who resonate with femme energy, regardless of gender identity, and to be inclusive to the greatest degree possible. While our language is inherently coded by the structures this book seeks to undermine and revolve, my aim has been to have intent and impact merge throughout for the inclusion and benefit of all.

As well, I write this book as a white cisgender able-bodied woman, straight-presenting while bending in the direction of bisexuality on the spectrum of sexual orientation, raised in a class trajectory that went from working to middle to upper-middle class over the course of my upbringing, highly educated, and bearing other significant stamps of privilege. I cannot claim to speak for those outside my realm of experience, but I do share within the book the stories and experiences of my clients across the spectrums of diversities that they represent.

At this moment in our collective history, this book seeks to confront in part the fact that white women urgently need to reconcile with our internalized racism and sexism, and our complicity in systems that perpetrate hate. I am relentless in my demand for that work and accountability. We are *too late* in confronting our complicity, and we are *too often* part of the problem rather than the solution. As a result, there are parts of this book that speak particularly to white women in stark terms on the work left to be done. I do not, in these portions of the book and in speaking explicitly to the ways in which white women need to confront our complicity with systems of oppression, mean to negate in any way whatsoever the incredible work of Black, brown, and Indigenous heroines on the path—past, present, and future—nor their lived experiences and critical role as heroines in all the revolutionary work currently under way. It is my hope that I have adequately

conveyed my belief that we must all walk arm in arm while following the lead of women of color if we are to achieve real change
and real redress for historic harm, and as we work to build a better world for all. Where the teachings of specific Black, brown,
and Indigenous women, men, and non-binary folx have impacted
my work, I have done my best to name them and to give all credit
where it is (long over)due.

Lastly, there are doubtless places in this book at which, through
the lens of history, my words will appear outdated and wrong,
where I will have to be accountable once again for blind spots in
my own thinking, and for which I will owe amends and apologies.
We are living right now in a portal of transformation that is so
rapid that this book has already had many lives and many incarna-
tions and at each stage has been revised over and over to become
more inclusive and, I hope, more reflective of my ever-growing
awareness of the work ahead. I have done my best throughout this
book to write from an anti-racist and anti-bias lens, from the moral
and ethical principles by which I live my own life, and to all those
across every spectrum of diversity with whom I walk on this beautiful and difficult path toward creating freedom and justice, and
with love, for all.

Section One

Recognition

1.

Awakening

I'm scrolling back more than ten years now—to a late Thursday evening when I was on my way out of work. I was the most senior woman associate in the litigation department of my Wall Street law firm. I walked through the security door for our grand offices with views over all of Manhattan, and out to the elevator bank on the thirty-fifth floor. There, I ran into Leonard, one of the senior partners.

Squat and with a gray beard, Leonard had been with the firm for something like forty years. I didn't know Leonard all that well. A few weeks prior, I'd been the second chair on a 350-million-dollar case he'd brought in—one where another senior woman and I ran the trial, while he sat in the first row and watched. I hadn't worked with him before that case.

As with many of the senior partners in the firm, however, there were stories about Leonard that floated around the office—tales

of his affair with a female partner in litigation a decade earlier—
an affair that, after a scandalous karaoke event at the firm Christmas party where he sang "I've Got You Babe" to his lover in front
of his wife, had resulted in that female partner's transfer to another division. This seemed to not have touched Leonard's career
at all. There were tales of his wife's (fairly understandable) insta-
bility, including an event where she screamed "Fuck you!" at her
husband in the middle of a celebratory dinner for an entire trial
team of lawyers, and then stormed out of the restaurant. And then
there was the more general fact that Leonard didn't seem to do
much but sit in his office for about five or six hours a day and col-
lect a massive salary and partnership draw, while the more junior
members of the firm struggled with eighty-hour weeks and 3 a.m.
emails.

In contrast to the workload of Leonard and many of the senior
partners at the firm, mine was merciless in both hours and commitment. My perfectionism as a lawyer had been well honed over
more than a dozen years of litigation and trial work. Along the
way, I'd gained a reputation for certain skill sets—for the ability to
precisely, relentlessly, and with stealthy questioning tear witnesses
apart under oath; for writing briefs that won the hardest motions;
and for a courtroom presence that opposing attorneys underestimated at their peril. Partners in other divisions came to me to write
pivotal motions in critical cases, against folks, for like a certain
high-profile New York real estate investor whose casinos in Atlantic City were in their third bankruptcy.

But I wasn't just invested in how I looked on paper. In my rare
spare time, I tore through every book I could find on women's
leadership, and did my best to put it all into practice. I was a net-

working fiend, a builder of alliances, and focused on growing my practice. I'd worked so hard in and on my career that I didn't finally decide to get married and think about starting a family until I was thirty-eight.

My work, in other words, was the aim and the dominant focus of my life.

Happiness was a different story. For a number of years preceding that fateful night at the elevator bank, I'd had the distinct sensation of beating my head against a brick wall, every single day. I'd put myself through law school, worked every day of my life since the age of fifteen, and checked every box presented to me as a metric of success—from taking on a triple major from a top tier college as an undergrad to wooing a major investment bank to my law firm as a potential client. Along the way, I'd immersed myself in feminist theory and cultural studies, and a love of activism that led me from organizing protests as a teenager to trying massive human rights cases pro bono in corporate law.

Despite all this understanding and awareness, despite all this hard work, I'd never been able to overcome what felt like a foot on the head of my success that I couldn't name. I spent years as a lawyer questing for the magic bullet that would finally get me the ease of ascension I saw in the careers of my male colleagues. When that failed, as it always did, I focused on being so good at the job that I couldn't be ignored (or so I thought). Overworking numbed the pain, and the dangling carrot of partnership kept me going.

So committed was I to this path that by the time I ran into Leonard at the elevator bank on that fateful Thursday night, I hadn't lost a case or a motion *in three years*.

And that particular night felt like a good night. My guard was down. The case I'd team-tried on behalf of Leonard's client a couple of weeks before had resulted in total victory. A few days after that, I'd won a pivotal motion in a major case. And that very day, minutes before heading to the elevator bank, I'd learned a judge had dismissed a case against my client based on a brief I'd written.

As we waited for the elevator to arrive, Leonard turned to me and said, "So how are you doing today?"

The bell dinged the elevator's arrival. I smiled at him as we boarded.

"We won the motion in that 10(b)(5) case today. That's three wins in a week. Feels pretty good."

Leonard barely smiled, and said nothing. When the elevator reached the ground floor, we stepped off and said goodnight.

It could have been any other bit of small talk, on any other night, with any other lawyer.

It was not that, but something very different.

A few days later, I was called into the office of the managing partner for the litigation division. Leonard had reported something "deeply troubling" to the partnership in a meeting that morning, and the managing partner wanted to ask me about it. Flummoxed, I asked what he meant.

"You've been accused of taking credit for the work of others," the managing partner said, point blank.

The room tilted a bit and I remember the brief sense that everything was a pale shade of green. My head spun. I racked my memory for possible events that could have been misinterpreted to fit this description. None came to mind.

"I don't know what you're talking about," I said as firmly as I could muster, my face getting hot. "And I would never do that. That's just not my style."

"That's surprising, because Leonard reported that you took credit for three victories in cases that other people worked on."

My stomach turned. "When does he think I did this?"

The managing partner stared at me from across the desk. "A few nights ago," he said, "in a conversation by the elevator bank."

My jaw dropped. He kept going.

"Elizabeth, I want to make something clear to you. This has raised a concern within the partnership as to whether you are too concerned with your own ambition, and perhaps don't understand your place within the department. Your work here is in service to the partners' clients, as a team player and at their discretion, not to benefit yourself or your own aims.

"I'm making a note of this for purposes of your annual review. We'll discuss how this event will impact your promotion potential at that time."

I was dumbstruck. I fumbled through a response about how I hadn't taken credit for anything—how I'd just remarked in passing that it felt good to be a part of three wins in a week, that it was just a passing conversation, small talk at the end of the night, and that I certainly would never discount the team effort on any case.

"That's not how Leonard reported it," he said. "Please consider what we've discussed and get back to work."

Six months later, the event at the elevator bank came up again in my promotion discussion, as well as in my salary and bonus review. I was offered a pittance of a bonus, and within a few weeks, the nearly all-male partnership committee decided that I just wasn't a good fit for the "team player mentality" required for promotion at the firm. (A coda: a male associate with six years less experience than I, a perpetually enormous ego, and a notorious reputation for inflating his billable hours got promoted in my stead.)

Where were the women, you may be wondering. In my department, there were two female equity partners. One was known for backing up the firm on everything, even policies that adversely impacted her own gender. She'd tell stories on panels about how exceptionally well treated she'd been during her maternity leave because she had performed, in her view, exceptionally, no matter how others complained that they were forced to work through their leave, and forced to work full-time hours thereafter even while being paid part-time. She had chaired the women's issues committee at the firm for a period of time. And whenever she was in the room, junior women held their tongues, afraid to discuss the truth of their experiences at the firm for fear that their tales of mistreatment would make their way to senior leadership, and then be held against them. The only other female equity partner was largely absent, both as an advocate and as a role model. She kept her head down, she did her work, and she didn't align herself with the concerns or needs of other women in the firm. In short, and in very typical ways that will be unpacked later on in this book, both were agents in preserving the status quo, rather than furthering change. I, like all the other younger women attorneys in the firm, was on my own.

Shortly after my bonus announcement and a few days before Christmas, I was advised that my career at the firm was likely over, though there was a nice severance package waiting for me as long as I agreed not to sue the firm for discrimination. I took the severance and walked away. I told only one person that I was pregnant by the time I left—the head of my department. In my exit interview, he thanked me for not raising that fact in my severance negotiations. Three days later, I learned that sometime during that last week at the firm, I'd had a silent miscarriage.

A lot has happened in the years since—growth, change, motherhood, newfound wisdom, and new work. But a residue remains from this series of events. What clings to me from those last, brutal days of full-time law practice, what hovers around me like an odor I can't entirely eliminate, is what I felt to be a total and complete powerlessness—that decisions were being made that would forever change the course of my life, simply because those with power decided that I did not, and should not, belong in their corridors.

What I have realized since is that, in a certain way, they were right. I did not belong there, because I was meant for something far greater than what they had promised but failed to deliver.

And though I felt I was being punished at the time—denied credit for my work, kept from the partnership I knew was well deserved, insulted, bullied, and dismissed—in reality, I was being handed a gift. It took me years to decode and reframe this opportunity, and it took *work*.

The question I began to ask myself more than ten years ago, as I started to unpack the messaging on success and change I'd received throughout my life, was *why* was I in this place, and why *now*?

JUST "LEAN IN" UNTIL YOU FALL OVER AND MAYBE THEN YOU'LL BE GOOD ENOUGH

For decades, commentators and purported "experts" on models of women's leadership tried to tell women how to navigate leadership and change.

We've been told how to dress, how to smile at the right moment, how to be not too assertive but just assertive enough.

We've been instructed on how to meet the male gaze, how to satisfy and embody male patterns of leadership, and how to not rock the boat with our own gifts and ambitions and needs.

We've been told how to quest for the corner office by acting like men, navigating career choices like men, how to speak and act like men, while not being too "masculine."

And we've been repeatedly told that if we did everything on this bucket list—every last bit of it—it would still be on us if we failed, because we had missed some random one last thing that was purportedly wrong with us individually that had failed to meet the mark.

All the while, as we sucked up this "advice," we were taught to distance ourselves from internal wisdom and from the nagging voices in our own heads that told us something wasn't right—even in the face of pay inequity or other forms of overt discrimination— and, above all, to avoid questioning whether maybe, just maybe, there were bigger issues at play than our own individual flaws.

Eventually, if you're like me, you've felt as though you were beating your head against a wall that wouldn't give, trying to find a way to make it work, trying to find the magic key that would open the door to that mythical idea known as "success."

The Seattle Public Library
Broadview Branch
Visit us on the Web: www.spl.org

Checked Out Items 2/16/2022 18:21
XXXXXXXXX3121

Item Title	Due Date
0010102043212	3/9/2022
Who is Alex Trebek? : a biography	
0010104330997	3/9/2022
Becoming heroines : unleashing our power for revolution and rebirth	

# of Items: 2

Renewals: 206-386-4190
TeleCirc: 206-386-9015 / 24 hours a day
Online: myaccount.spl.org

Pay your fines/fees online at pay.spl.org

There's a lot out there claiming to be that magic key. If you're like me, you've read everything you can get your hands on related to the topic broadly known as "women's leadership"—and trust me on this, at a certain point it all starts to blur together. In our quest to try to figure out why we can't get ahead and why we're never or rarely happy, we've been asked to analyze some questions: Do we need to be more of a "girl boss" or a "boss bitch"? Maybe we need to be more "corner office." Maybe we just need to "think like a man." Maybe if we just "lean in" a little harder, a little more, show up for one more event, network perfectly with one more person, placate one more client or boss, smile more, put up with the occasional racist or sexist or homophobic remark, the momentary or pervasive sexual harassment, and the refusal to see us as anything other than, well, less than, and, don't forget, to evaluate and self-criticize every gesture, every angle, every aspect of our bodies, voices, hairstyles, laughter, laugh lines, outfit and shapewear choices, and on and on and on, maybe finally we'll be able to satisfy the demands of those with authority over us.

Or maybe, after years of this internal and external struggle, we conclude that in the end the problem is *us*, so why bother.

What I've come to realize in the years since I left those spaces for greener pastures is that the end game of structures of power and oppression is exactly *that* aim—to silence us, to keep us just off-kilter enough to not fight back, to keep us striving to meet arbitrary and ever-shifting standards by which to measure our value, to cause us to compete with one another for an ever-shrinking pie, and most importantly, to cause us to deny our gifts and thereby fail to organize and create change—epic, structure-overturning, revolutionary, world-altering change—from the inside out.

I'm here to present you with a radical notion, one that others have spoken about but that we all must now internalize as we begin the journey of Becoming Heroines:

> We fail not because we aren't good enough.
> We fail because our failure preserves the status quo.
> And perhaps even more importantly, we fail because we are meant for better than this.

When we are able to burn the myths that got us here, and to confront the reality of the structures designed to give only a small group of us power, with strategies that will *change* the status quo *forever*, we become heroines for ourselves; for women we know, love, and work with; and for those coming up the ladder behind us and in the world at large.

IT'S NOT YOU, IT'S WHITE SUPREMACIST PATRIARCHY

In my day job, I'm now the CEO of a company dedicated to world-changing leadership, with a particular focus on cultivating heroines in women's leadership. Day in and day out, I work with women and non-binary folx—and a few good men—who are trying to meet ever-changing goalposts that will allow them to survive and achieve. Despite working inside some of the world's largest companies, I'm perpetually surprised by how many of us are without the language or the understanding of how power functions to keep us from just getting by, let alone thriving.

Sure, many of us understand the idea of patriarchy: that our culture is designed to give cis men power and to preserve that power once obtained, while excluding women, LGBTQ+ folx, and non-binary people from attaining it. We also may understand and feel the impact of white supremacy—that incredibly pervasive myth that white people are better than all others, built as it is into every aspect of our society, and structured to benefit those who are white to the detriment of—directly and often violently—Black, brown, and Indigenous people.

And while we might be able to describe a few or lots of instances in which we know patriarchy and/or white supremacy played out in our own lives, we may lack the language to describe how they function in every moment of every day, and even in our own thinking, to keep us down.

And worse still, we may fail to understand how these systems of power operate *through* us—how they work to make us enforcers of oppression even as we are also its victims.

White supremacist patriarchy functions in four key ways:

Systemic Oppression: our society is built to benefit white straight cisgender able-bodied men to the detriment of all others.

Institutional Oppression: our institutions—government, criminal justice, law, medicine, and virtually all corporate or nonprofit institutions—are rooted in systemic oppression and thereby working to further it, absent conscious rebellion against its norms.

Interpersonal Oppression: by and between each other, we execute and maintain the norms of oppression on a spectrum from overt harm, such as sexual violence or racist assaults, to microaggressions designed to maintain the status quo through shame, guilt, or worthlessness perpetrated in conscious and unconscious ways.

Internalized Oppression: as products of systemic, institutional, and interpersonal oppression, we internalize messages of otherness, and enforce them upon ourselves through self-sabotage, self-abuse, negative internal messaging—and yes, it should be said, through leadership books by authors who fail to recognize their role in enforcing and perpetrating patriarchal and white supremacist norms in the guise of "helping" women and others to "succeed."

This book is here to teach you how to fight back against all of this, from the smallest thought in your own head to the gravest systemic injustices, and in the process to become a heroine in your own life, for others, and in the world. It is here to teach you how to bring the rain in your own life, so that nothing stands in the way of your goddess-given role in helping to build a more equitable and just world for all of us.

I'm here to present to you now the four stages of your own heroine's journey, designed to give you exactly that.

Recognition: Recognition begins with a moment of profound and conscious awareness that something must change, and that the status quo must shift. This is a pivot point of awakening that catalyzes us to begin to want to shout truth to power, even if the cost is quite high. Immediately, we confront the silencing, loss, and limitations that have been imposed upon us by patriarchy and white supremacy, and how that has impacted us in the most public and the most intimate ways, including in the stories that we tell ourselves about our own worthiness and the nature of our ability to lead. Here, we begin to find our gifts and our voice as we grasp our own leadership. Here, we begin to speak truth to power.

Recognition is a tool against internalized oppression that, if cultivated over time, dismantles the damage done within ourselves.

Reconciliation: As the heroine's journey continues, we are called to confront the damage that has been done to us, and the damage that has been done to others by and through us.

Reconciliation calls us to confront our trauma and our privilege, and to begin to do the work of understanding how our internalized biases have impacted the end goals of our work as women leaders. Reconciliation begins the process of heroines becoming co-conspirators across intersectional lines in a quest for justice.

Throughout this process, we learn that it is important for us to listen before we speak, to engage in difficult conversations, to commit to growth and equity in all that we do, even when it's messy and imperfect. It is in this trajectory that we learn to become comfortable with discomfort as a force for good, and to continue on the heroine's journey toward real change. We are challenged to off-load our trauma, heal our wounds, and hand back to structures of oppression the baggage and the weaponry that was never ours to carry.

Reconciliation is a tool against interpersonal oppression, one that carries with it a profound opportunity for healing across all women and in the world.

Revolution: Revolution is the place where we take the lessons we have learned from the work of Recognition and Reconciliation, and activate to change politics, policy, and the personal to create a world that is equitable and free for all of us. Having done the internal work of confronting our silencing, loss, and trauma, and having begun the process of addressing the damage we've done to others as tools to reinforce oppression, we are enabled to begin to create concrete change for ourselves and for others—at work, at home, and in the world. We become allies for others and advocates for ourselves as we activate to change the world collectively.

Revolution is a tool against institutional oppression, where we collectively and actively work to change, shift, and sometimes overthrow the institutions that have operated to perpetrate harm, including at the personal, professional, and societal levels.

Rebirth: Rebirth, finally, is the place where heroines emerge to claim our power. In this moment of revolution that we are currently living through, many of us have imagined a world where equity and justice are fully realized, and what that might look like. Here, we have power. Here, we declare our rights as *we* define them. Here, we create a world for all of us, listening and leading in collective, through imperfect but committed growth toward our ideals. We set equitable expectations and work to embody them. We strive daily to create a future of freedom for all, for ourselves and as a legacy for our children, our places of work, and our culture, even if we may not see it fully realized in our lifetimes. We find joy. We begin again and always on the path of the heroine, for as long as it takes.

Rebirth is a tool against systemic oppression, where we set new paradigms for culture and society, and we set about building them every day, for as long as the journey lasts.

In this world that we are striving to create, our capacity to envision it predicts our ability to live into it. What we choose to design together *now* will predict the world we live in for centuries to come. That future is dependent on the healing and the rebirth of heroines everywhere, from the inside out.

WAIT, WHAT HAVE I GOTTEN MYSELF INTO HERE?

At this point, you may be wondering what this book is *really* all about. Perhaps you picked it up looking for yet another silver bullet to get you to the top of the traditional leadership pile. Perhaps the word *revolution* is a little frightening, even if it's grounded in the idea of revolving and evolving the systems and institutions that cause harm to ourselves and others.

Stick with me.

As you continue forward in this book, I'd like you to consider the possibility that women's leadership is not *actually* about our own personal success, though that's the metric that's been put forward.

I'd like you to consider instead the possibility that true women's leadership is about how we collaborate to change the world.

Because here's the thing: so long as the realm of "women's leadership" lives within the dominant paradigm set by men, so long as we view our role in the world as one that has to catch up to metrics that don't apply to us and never have, so long as we define success according to standards that we didn't write and that have never worked for us, we will never, in the end, be successful, nor will we manage to address every inequity still present in the world in which we live.

The existing system is designed for us to fail, so that it can survive.

What we need, in other words, is a new system. My view is that the role of women leaders, *as heroines*, is to create that system.

Our success, moreover, is inherently dependent on each of us using and recognizing the gifts that we bring to the table as tools for change, and through an intersectional lens that benefits all of us.

Absent that, we will never be able to truly envision and create models of leadership that benefit *everyone*, not just a chosen few. Absent that, we're destined to continue striving to satisfy systems of oppression that need our failure—or capitulation to the status quo, like those few women partners with whom I once worked— in order to continue to succeed.

If you're doubting me, I'd just ask you which is better: 1) continuously hunting for magic bullets to satisfy those in power, whose maintenance of power depends on our failure, or 2) choosing instead to become a force for change to create a world that allows all of us to have and share in power, and defining *that* as a true metric of success? I know which one sounds better to me.

Lastly, I want to acknowledge that you are probably exhausted as you are reading this. There is not a single woman I know who has lived through the recent events we've experienced in the United States and worldwide who is not bone tired. With that upheaval, of course, came real moments of exhilaration, joy, and hard-won victories that kept us on the path, along with profound and lasting loss matched only by collective grief.

Even still, significant factions of those in power are counting on your fatigue. Those in power are counting on you to quit. Keep reading. Keep going. We're all going to get there together.

The results of choosing to do this work will touch every aspect of your life—from the smallest choices you make in your most intimate relationships, to the big-picture choices that change your life completely. Confronting internalized oppression is akin to ripping back the veil on the lessons that we've been taught since childhood. As with the lessons we've learned in the valley of the shadow of death, once those structures of oppression are seen, it's impossible to stuff them back behind the veil and return to the way things were before.

As I've proceeded through my own investigation, I've gone through cycles of grief, loss, and rage. As you examine how your trajectory and the trajectories of others have been dramatically and artificially limited, your gifts squelched, and your purpose made elusive, you may experience this as well. I'm going to encourage you along the way to convert those profound and important emotional realizations into insight and into action.

I've worked with thousands of women through the processes I'm sharing with you. The awakening is always and inevitably profound, moving, and sometimes terrifying. Notably, it's not always about what we choose to move toward, but also about what we choose to leave behind. My aim in this book is to invite you to rise to become the heroine that lives within you, with an understanding that there are smaller and larger steps along the path.

From finding the courage to revolt against structures of harm, to using your voice for change, to leaving an abusive marriage or job, to working to create first-ever best-practices policies for inclusion within your organization, real change is possible when we off-load the baggage of white supremacist patriarchy within ourselves and get to work on changing relationships, institutions, and whole systems that have refused to move forward to benefit us—or leave them behind in the dust, because that, too, is progress.

The change that comes for you as a result of this book will depend on how you choose to use what is offered here, and where. Indeed, one of the great joys of doing the work that I do is that I get to see how all those I work with are propelled out into the world as a result of it, to use their unique skills and voice for change. I can guarantee you, however, that the process of uncovering the heroine within will shift your life, your work, and the world for the better. Along the way, you'll cultivate new, freer, and more supportive relationships; you'll be compelled to create change in all the spaces you occupy; you'll build allies in and for the battles ahead to better the world; and you'll see your true self emerge completely, as the heroine you are meant to become.

BUT WAIT! WHAT IF I'M NOT READY FOR THIS?!

So here's the thing: we're living in extraordinary times. What we've been through in the last five years alone has been more than any of us expected to live through in a lifetime. Right now, at this moment in history, everyone is called to contribute, and all our gifts are needed. Whether you are ready or not, you must begin.

Opportunities for radical change like the one presented to us right now do not come along all that often. We must dig deep, get to the root of our fears, work to heal generations of harm, and prepare ourselves to move beyond our histories. Those of us who have been complicit with structures of oppression have a chance to make amends and to tear down those structures arm in arm with those harmed by them. Those of us who have experienced harm and been denied power have a chance to take power and lead. Those of us who have denied ourselves and our deepest desires have a chance to claim who we really are. Wherever we have privilege we must leverage and seek to undermine it. Wherever we do not, we must kick in the door and claim our seat at the table.

It is my belief that the world needs transformative thinking at all levels, and revolutionaries of all kinds. As the last few years have shown, artists can create change as much as politicians and activists—think about the work of Manuel Oliver, for instance, who lost a child in the Parkland massacre and turned his art into activism against gun violence in memory of his son. Music can move us to confront our historic traumas as much as a speech in a courtroom can compel justice, as the Resistance Revival Chorus has shown us over and over. Gardeners, shamans, lawyers, teachers, even bankers and movers of capital can do their work with greater compassion and bravery in this moment—we all can, each according to her gifts and desires, and if we choose to tap into them fully. We must use all the tools and structures of the world that we have available to us—many of them imperfect—and we must also create new and more responsive ones along the way, as I discuss in later sections of this book.

Even if we do not feel we are ready, starting now is demanded, I believe, by all those who have come before us, by all the deep

and magnificent work of people who have been historically marginalized, by those heroes and heroines we call ancestors who
stand as examples for all of us in so many ways. There is a clarion
call for all of us to now move forward together, to break through,
arm in arm, across every diversity, to create a world that is free
and just and equitable for all of us. My personal belief is that we
have all incarnated on the planet at this time with a job to do, and
we all need to do it—right now, and as quickly as possible.

Now is our time, and we must claim it.

2.

The Match
Set Aflame

I t was around 4 a.m. on the morning of November 9, 2016, that I realized I was going to have to tell my kids that Donald Trump had won the election. I was on the floor of my bathroom, having vomited until I was left with nothing but dry heaves. I sat there, crying, trying to figure out what was coming next, knowing all the way down into my bones that whatever it was would be unimaginably horrific.

The night before, we'd ventured out in our Brooklyn neighborhood to the intersection of two streets named President and Clinton. I'd taken video on my phone of my four-year-old daughter shouting "smash the patriarchy!" The prior morning, I'd taken both kids with me to vote for Hillary, after having done everything I could as a single mother of two young children to get her elected.

That fall wasn't just a profoundly political time for me—it was also personal. I'd separated from my kids' dad in September. Indeed, the last family photo of us was taken on the morning of the 2016 election, outside my polling place.

But in the breaking dawn of the following day, on the floor of that bathroom, realizing what had happened with Trump's election and compounded by the other awful things I'd already had to tell my kids in recent days, I was wracked with grief.

As the sun came up, I crawled back into my bed with both kids. My son was the first to wake up. He was three at the time, the sweet, peaceful demeanor that reflects his hugely compassionate heart already on full display.

When I told him Donald Trump had won the election, he sat up in bed, stared at me, and started to cry. "Is he going to be a good man now?" he asked. "Is he going to stop grabbing girls?" The bewilderment in his little face, the fat tears rolling down his little cheeks, flat out broke me.

And the shock of that moment broke many of us. I have said many times since that the thing about that moment for so many women is that we knew—maybe not consciously, but we knew—the absolutely craven, revolting nature of what was to come—that it would be hateful, violent, a descent into madness and mass death for this country and the world. We knew on some level that it would be worse than we could even at that moment imagine. We knew.

Later that morning, after I'd dropped my kids at daycare, the process of coming to terms began.

This was not the first time I'd encountered a reckoning like this. I'd organized my first protest as a teenage summer student at Harvard to try to get the university to divest from South Africa during apartheid. As a college student, after organizing anti-rape protests on campus, I'd decided to sue the man who had molested me as a teenager—a circumstance that I'll discuss later on in the book when we talk about confronting trauma. As a young attorney, after a senior co-counsel publicly compared me to a whore at a business dinner, I'd decided to go to my boss and to then refuse to engage with that co-counsel publicly in meetings in any way—a choice that resulted in a comment in my performance review while ongoing business between my firm and that co-counsel continued with no consequence.

Countless times I'd been forced by fate or happenstance into moments of having to *choose* whether to capitulate or whether to fight. Those moments are, in a word, a match that starts a fire, an ember that leads to a blaze. The night of the 2016 election set alight the lives of millions of women, changing perceptions, burning myths they'd relied on their whole lives, changing their values and their choices forevermore, and setting them on the path of the heroine.

WHAT IS THE MATCH?

The Match is a moment in one's own life—or for that matter, the life of organizations, companies, and nations—where what was tolerable suddenly becomes intolerable, and where we are then forced to choose: live with what can't be lived with, or rise to fight. You will recognize the Match in your own life as you think back on moments when you *knew* things had to change. And to be clear, the Match is not your ordinary should I or shouldn't I— should I take this job, should I ask for more money, should I speak out about what happened in today's meeting.

No, the Match is usually set aflame from trauma—an emotional, physical, or spiritual injury that marks us in ways we cannot deny. In my experience, the Match usually lights after a single catastrophic event or a series of ever-increasing ones. Sometimes a barely noticeable series of pinpricks that eventually become just one too many is what fires up the Match. A point is struck that forces us to choose: Am I willing to go on like this?! If not, what am I going to do about it?!

Think of the pilot light on a gas stove—the *click click click* when you turn the knob, the moment in between the turn and when you're waiting for the gas to light. For me, there is always a millisecond of choice: Will it catch, or won't it? That space is the moment that is cultivated by the Match: when we decide whether, and how, we will set our lives on fire, and run toward a different future, no matter what it takes.

You should be warned that once the Match lights, it often burns so hot it can't be extinguished. Like the Silverado fire, it may tear through the hills of your life, rendering everything ashes. In other circumstances, it may be a small spark that burns for a while before taking light. But trust this: it will continue to burn until what has been lit is addressed. This is one reason, by the way, why the path of the heroine is never one you can step off of completely once you've stepped on. Matches light the fire, an aspect of our life begins to transform, and there's no going back.

That is not to say that Matches are welcome moments in our personal or political history. As you'll see in this chapter, sometimes they are born of profound loss. Uniformly, however, they bring with them the intolerable sense that *something must change*.

It is the Match that causes us to leave abusive marriages after we've been hit that one last time when we've been promised it would never happen again. It is the Match that causes us to quit jobs that fail to promote us for the fourth and final time. It is the Match that causes us to report the come-on from a boss, or to canvass our neighbors for our preferred candidate, or to start whole political movements, because *we have finally had enough.*

It is the Match that turns ordinary women into activists and leaders. It is the Match that leads us to *refuse* to put up with hate, racism, sexism, oppression, indignity for one moment longer, and instead to turn and fight.

And in my experience, it is usually an enormous amount of pain, grief, rage, or fear that turns the Match into a flame, and the flame into action.

LIGHTING THE MATCH IN YOUR OWN LIFE

In the course of my work as a women's leadership coach, I've met thousands of women who are in points of crisis—where a Match has been lit, and they know that things can't go on, but they're unsure of where to go next. As mentioned above, when confronted by that moment, there are really only two questions to ask:

1. Am I willing to let things continue as they are?
2. If I'm not, what am I going to do about it?

Which brings me to a necessary corollary: if the answer to the first question is no, the fire within you will always call upon you to do things you have never done before, that are outside your comfort zone, that may terrify you.

Changing your workplace, changing culture, even changing *yourself* isn't easy. And one of the keys to propelling through that moment of fire, to beginning to confront the question "What am I going to do about it?" is to get used to the idea that *it will be uncomfortable.* It is impossible to create a better world, a better job, or a better life without becoming comfortable in discomfort.

We've been trained to run from discomfort a lot. Patriarchy has taught us for centuries to placate, play nice, stay silent, be polite, and not rock the boat—and believe me, we're going to confront those mindsets in coming chapters.

For now, though, consider whether you're willing to tolerate discomfort to get to a better place. Are you willing to consider that your boss might not like you if you ask him to confront the racial or gender inequities in your workplace? Are you willing to consider that members of your family might not like you if you step forward to organize a protest against racism or crushing blows to reproductive choice? Are you willing to put your own comfort on the line to just explore the question, asked in the most intolerable parts of your life and the world, "What am I going to do about it?"

If you're willing, then you've chosen to set your life aflame. You've met the Match and returned to it the spark of your willingness to change and to create change.

Please note that this choice is not one and done, though. At every new stage of the heroine's journey, you'll be asked to confront new levels of discomfort on the path to growth. Think, for example, of the training that it took to build warriors of legend and myth. Days, months, years of physical, emotional, spiritual training that at every stage asked the hero or heroine for more, deeper, better, even when every limit had already been pushed. On the path to becoming heroines, we will be challenged over and over and over again to confront our own limitations—both self-imposed, and culturally imposed—and to push through the discomfort that is required to *grow*. This is not easy work, but it is necessary, and usually unavoidable.

Because the secret about the Match and its ascendant fire, you see, is this: there is no way out but through.

WALKING THE TERROR FIELD

About a dozen years ago, at a workshop at a small entrepreneurs' collective, I was introduced to the idea of "the terror field." Though I have tried many times over the years to locate the origin of this notion, I've been unable to trace it back to any source. However, the truth of its message has worked time and again with clients as they process their response to a lit Match that they're confronting in their own lives.

The concept of the terror field goes like this: in any new path we are charting in life or in the world, as we approach that new path, our terror level will begin to increase. The closer we get to a new level of change, success, challenge, or growth, the more terrified we will become. What if we fail? What if we're rejected? What if we have no idea what we're doing? Those questions will not only increase but also become more dominant in our thinking.

This is what happens when you're crossing the terror field: the closer you get to the goal, the more afraid you become.

The key, however, is this: *keep going.*

A fundamental quality of the terror field as it was explained to me is this: if we can push through our terror to the end goal, the next time we are challenged, navigating the terror field will be easier.

However, the inverse is also true: if we turn away from our fear, and retreat to safer territory, the next time we step onto the terror field, it will be *worse, harder, more frightening than before,* because we opted not to keep going the last time.

Indeed, this is a key feature of confronting an incendiary Match and sitting in inquiry with "What am I going to do about it?"—terror is a part of the game. (And for some of us, that fear is really a matter of life or death. If I confront the police who murdered my son, will they come for me next?)

And a brief note here: there is a difference between fear for one's physical or emotional safety and fear that limits us from pushing toward a choice we know we are destined to make. The terror field is not about jeopardizing your safety, health, or wellness. It *is* about the fear of the unknown, however, and the willingness to challenge yourself to strive toward the best version of yourself, your life, your leadership, and your world.

I want to assure you of one thing, however: no one who has ever stepped onto the path of the heroine has been without fear. Indeed, the strongest women I know will tell you that fear is a friend, sometimes a warning, sometimes noise in the background, but most of the time just a constant companion. As with discomfort, accepting the challenge of the Match is also a willingness to face your fear *and keep going anyway.*

An aspect of confronting a Match, then, is a question of weight:

Does the need for change outweigh anxiety? Does the irrefutable demand to alter the world, your workplace, your life for the better matter more than fear? Does the need to make a difference now, to confront all that brought you to this moment and make it better, matter more than your own internal field of terror? *Are you willing to face the fear and do it anyway?*

You know the answer. That's why you're here.

In the next few chapters, I'm going to show you how to confront the voices and limitations in your own head and in the world that have kept all of us at times from pushing forward to create change—that have caused us to turn back on the field of terror, to retreat, to hide, and to wait.

I'm going to do that because a key component of the journey to becoming heroines is this: when you change the inner, you change the outer. When you change your internal limitations and beliefs, you change your outward-facing actions and your capacity to create good. When you change the way you've internalized oppression, you alter radically your ability to fight it in the world. When you change yourself, you create the capacity for change everywhere.

And this, in the end, is the point of a lit Match wherever we find it, welcome or not, in trauma or not, and in the face of the most grievous losses: with tools, community, and effort, we can shift trauma into healing, pain into justice, and words into action.

This is how we step onto the path: we choose to step forward, toward change, come what may.

ONWARD

Perhaps you are one of the women who lit a Match on the night of the 2016 election. Perhaps you lit one decades earlier, and have been using your voice for change ever since. Perhaps, like me, you've been confronted over and over again by the appearance of a Match in your own life, personally, professionally, politically. No matter. We will journey along this path together.

As we walk our individual terror fields and explore the biggest questions of our lives on the path to becoming heroines, as we consider the fires through which we've walked to get here and how they have demanded that we create change, please know that the only way we succeed is with one another. We'll talk more about that, too, in the coming chapters, but for now, I want you to remember that when you are afraid, when you are uncomfortable, when you are uncertain, there are thousands of heroines with you on the path.

Here's to lighting a Match and cultivating the flame. Onward.

3.

Limits and Loss

Once the Match is struck, and we realize things have to change, we may find almost instantly that we run up against our own internal limitations. When I'm speaking in public and I am asked to identify the most common struggle of the women I've worked with, the answer is breathtakingly easy. Next to institutionalized sexism and other forms of discrimination—more on that in later parts of this book—virtually every woman I've worked with struggles with the voices in her own head that hold her back.

Take, for example, my client, an Indigenous woman, who built a massive media platform from the ground up. After years of being overlooked for funding and awards, she confronted her own moment of having had enough. Almost instantly, however, she ran up against voices in her own head that asked her if she *really* belonged in this industry, if she *really* deserved to be seen as an icon, if she *really* could claim the legacy that she had plainly already built.

The answer, of course, was yes. But first, to get to where she knew she needed to go, she, like all of us, needed to confront the voices within her claiming otherwise—voices that had been imprinted through cultural messaging, systemic oppression, and her own life experiences.

For some of us, these voices questioning our worthiness may not be at all conscious. What we say to ourselves in the mirror, while driving to work, while sitting in the boardroom or in a meeting in our community, may sound to us like the simple flow of critical thoughts. We may believe this is normal—just a part of the way our minds work and nothing more—even when those narratives are fundamentally a pattern of self-abuse and limitation.

One of the hardest things about working with powerful women who talk to themselves in ways that they would never tolerate in friends or colleagues is hearing what those voices actually say. For so many of us, the way that we talk to ourselves is downright awful. What we also don't realize, however, is that it is *optional*, not mandatory, and not *necessary*.

When we are regularly telling ourselves that we don't belong, that we are ugly or broken, that we'll never succeed, that we don't know what we're doing, that we deserved to be mistreated, that the abuse of a partner or boss is actually our fault, that we just have to work harder, lean in, do more, *be* more in order to succeed, we are—let me make it very plain—*lying* to ourselves.

What we're actually doing in real time is struggling with limiting beliefs—beliefs that have been imprinted on us through cultural oppression and/or through traumatic or emotional experiences that have hardened into worldviews about what's possible for us.

Many authors have written about limiting beliefs and their

impact on us. What has never been effectively answered, however, is this: How can we truly overcome them?

That's what this chapter is here to explore.

THE BOARD OF DIRECTORS

When I talk to clients about the messages flying around in their thoughts, it's helpful to apply a metaphor, namely what I call the Board of Directors.

Imagine that your thoughts are governed by a Board of Directors—an eclectic group of characters that have *very* vociferous opinions on how you should lead your life. Perhaps these are people you've known in your life—mothers and fathers are frequent characters on the Board of Directors—but they may also be unique aspects of your personality that sometimes try to run the show.

Members of your Board of Directors can at times be very loud in their opinions. "You'll never get that job," one might shout inside your head when you come across a position you've wanted forever. "There are hundreds of people more qualified for that than you." Another might pick a fight with your partner on your anniversary, starting with "She just doesn't appreciate all that I do in this partnership. Who does she think she is?"

Critically, there's one key aspect of the opinions of every member of the Board of Directors, one that may seem counterintuitive at first: your Board of Directors is there *to try to keep you safe*. Whether from shame, pain, failure, or other negative experiences, all our limiting beliefs have at their core the intention that if we follow them, we'll keep ourselves from getting hurt.

Moreover, every member of your Board of Directors has a shadow side and a light side. The voice that tells you not to go out for that ideal job is trying to protect you from rejection (light). The flip side, however, is that not applying for the job will limit your advancement (shadow). And if you listen to that voice over and over again, what is intended as protection leads to a pattern of limitation, stagnation, and a denial of your purpose and the impact that you can have as the heroine you are meant to be.

A first step to working with one's Board of Directors, then, is to recognize what those various aspects of our personalities are trying to do. Let me give you an example.

I have a member of my personal Board of Directors who I have come to refer to affectionately as Landmine Lizzie. The origin of this particular aspect of my personality is grounded in experiences I had as a child where my boundaries were routinely violated (and not to worry, we're going to talk about mining the origins of your own Board of Directors in a minute). As a result of those experiences, a very vocal limiting belief was cemented in my personality: "if you do not immediately respond to any incursion on your boundaries, bad, bad shit is going to happen to you."

In other words, I have an absolute hair-trigger temper when I witness anything that feels like an incursion on my personal or professional boundaries. Indeed, when Landmine Lizzie runs the show, I literally see green for a minute before lashing out over a perceived personal injustice.

I've been working consciously with this aspect of my personality for at least fifteen years. What I've come to learn about Landmine Lizzie is that she is actually trying very hard to protect the wounded child I used to be, who experienced so much trauma as a little girl without recognizing that as an adult, being a human landmine in relationships might have a really nasty cost. In other words, and to reframe this in light and shadow terms: the light side of Landmine Lizzie is that she wants to protect the little girl within from additional harm. The shadow side is that she's a bitch and a half to others and so quick to become enraged that she can be terrifying and destructive to relationships when unleashed.

So how do we unpack the origins of these personalities and belief structures so that we can consciously manage them and recognize them when they start to try to run the show? That's what we're turning to next. But before we do that, a quick word on limiting beliefs.

WHAT IS A LIMITING BELIEF?

In general, our Board of Directors speaks in the language of limiting beliefs, and is most often provoked when we are scared, angry, or threatened. If you find yourself in a cycle where you can't escape a certain line of thinking and you are frustrated, angry, afraid, or feel unable to change your circumstances, it's worth your time to consider whether you're living in the place of limiting beliefs. Notably, limiting beliefs live in the language of absolutism. If the voice in your head, for instance, is using the language of "always" or "never," chances are good you're dealing with a limiting belief.

A few examples:

"I'm never going to be able to retire because I'm bad with money."

"I guess I should just marry this person because it's not like there are a lot of options for women who look like me/are my age/ are my size/are divorced/are single moms/etc."

"After you get to SVP, it's always men who get promoted to the higher positions. That's just how it works. I might as well get used to it."

"There's no point in trying to push management to adopt a flextime policy so I can work from home one day a week. This place will never change."

"I'll never be able to pick up where I left off in my profession now that I've taken time off to have a kid, so why bother even trying?"

"This is just how the world/this business/this marriage/this industry works, so why bother trying to change it?"

You'll note that it's painful to read some of these. I've had women unload dozens of pages of limiting beliefs in coaching work that contain statements we say to ourselves that we would never tolerate another human being saying out loud to anyone else. Again, a reminder: as you'll soon learn, limiting beliefs are grounded in prior messaging, both culturally and in traumatic and discriminatory experiences, that crafts and solidifies our thinking as a means of protecting us from harm.

But there's another feature of limiting beliefs that you should be familiar with before we proceed, namely the phenomenon of "confirmation bias." Confirmation bias is a documented phenomenon whereby our minds, once settled on a particular belief about the way the world works, see our day-to-day experience through the lens of that belief, and reject evidence that undermines it. An example:

Let's say you have identified a belief that is kicking around in your head to the effect that "No one respects me at my job because I went to college later than everyone else here, and got a late start in this profession." On a given Friday morning, you email your boss asking for feedback on your latest project. Your boss doesn't reply. By Friday night, you've got a Board member screaming in your ear about how your boss doesn't respect you enough to even answer an email for a whole damn day, and you're never going to get ahead at the gig because you're too old, and you can't believe that yet again you're being mistreated.

You're in the middle of confirmation bias. How so? Well, your brain has taken your boss's non-response, run it through your limiting belief that you're never going to be respected at your job because you went to college later than everyone else, and decided to take that non-response as evidence that shores up your limiting belief.

In reality, your boss has been offline all day because he's been dealing with a sick parent, in a hospital with shitty reception. His failure to respond to your email had *nothing to do with you whatsoever.*

Confirmation bias causes us to create stories to understand our experiences through the lens of our already ingrained beliefs. When we begin to consider evidence that contradicts our limiting beliefs, however, we disable them—more on that in a minute.

For now, however, we're going to get to work on origins, because the key to getting to the bottom of our limiting beliefs is to understand how they were formed in the first place.

UNPACKING THE VOICES IN OUR HEADS: ORIGIN WORK

As we begin to explore our limiting beliefs and Board of Directors in detail, I have to warn you that this can be nasty work. Going deep into the grit of how we talk to ourselves reveals the ways in which we perpetrate abuse on ourselves and replicate the patterns of oppression, sexism, mistreatment, and violence we've experienced at the hands of others.

At the outset, and before I share with you the exercises that I've used with thousands of clients to dig at the underpinnings of this self-abuse, I have a request: be kind to yourself through this process. Reward yourself as you progress through it with physical and emotional nourishment—dark chocolate, playing with your dog, snuggles with your kids, maybe a Zoom date with a friend. If at any point the work feels overwhelming, take a break, and return to it in a day or two. And most importantly, don't try to do it all at once—because you couldn't, even if you tried.

Key to understanding this work is knowing that our personalities and thought patterns have taken a lifetime to build, and peeling back the layers of how and when certain belief structures were formed is an ongoing process. Just last week, I confronted another round of this work in my own thinking on money and abundance when I realized that messaging I received around money as a child—namely the idea that women are "bad with money"—had taken root in my thinking once again. I sat down for another round of writing and contemplation on this topic to consider how my thoughts were impacting my actions in terms of saving and paying off debt, causing me to run from more conscious money management because of my fear of "being bad at it." All of us are works in progress. The work I'm sharing with you here is designed to last a lifetime, and the tools within it are ones you'll apply over and over again.

So, to begin our origin work that digs at the root of how our limiting beliefs are formed, I'm going to ask you to pick one limiting belief or one member of your Board of Directors that you can easily identify. Just one, not more than one, or you'll get overwhelmed. Write down the limiting belief or the identity of the member of the Board of Directors at the top of a piece of paper or in a document on your laptop (note: humor helps—Landmine Lizzie was so designated because the name allowed me to laugh at what I perceived to be one of the worst aspects of my personality) and prepare to get to work.

Next, please sum up in one sentence the primary message of this limiting belief or Board member. You'll note, for instance, that with Landmine Lizzie, the primary message is "If you don't defend yourself the instant a line of any kind is crossed, you'll be in for a world of hurt." Give it some thought, and write down the primary belief in which this particular limiting belief or Board member is grounded.

And then, I'm going to ask you to answer what should be a simple question, but never is: What's the first time you can remember believing this statement to be true?

If you're anything like me, chances are good that as you sit reading this, instantly a memory springs to mind, and perhaps even one that has caused you to burst into tears—a memory of an event where, as a result of trauma, violence, abuse, or harm, something that was said or done to you that left a profound mark, you concluded that your absolutist limiting belief was true. Chances are this memory in and of itself is so painful it's hard to look at.

Write that memory down. All of it. Write down the event, the details, the feelings you had at the time, every single thing associated with it that is indelible in your memory. Write until you know you're done (and you'll know, whether it's a paragraph or ten pages, because you'll have the sense that you've "emptied it out" of your-self). And then I want you to note a couple of key things about the event:

- How old were you when it happened?
- Did you blame yourself for the event or did someone blame you?
- Can you identify how the belief was built in response to that event to protect you?
- Are you willing to believe that you will never have to live through an event like that ever again?
- Are you willing to trust that you do not need the limiting belief to keep yourself, at this stage in your own heroine's journey, safe?

And then lastly, I want you to take a good look at what you've written, and ask yourself some difficult questions: is the memory (or memories) of the event you've described rooted in discrimina-tion, bigotry, sexism? Is it associated with a stereotype, structure, or belief system that is designed to keep you in a certain place, to deny your gifts, to make you feel less than? Can you identify how the messaging that resulted from this event might have impacted your beliefs about what is possible for you by perpetrating the message that there is something inherently wrong with you be-cause of your gender, your race, your orientation, your ability sta-tus—because of who you are?

If so, I'm going to invite you to consciously give that baggage back.

This is the point in this book where I get to tell you that sys-tems of oppression give us burdens to bear that often manifest into limiting beliefs, and that that bullshit is *not our baggage to carry.* Let me give you some examples to clarify what I mean.

I've worked with countless women over the years, for instance, who were told at some point that girls are bad at math, or bad at science, or bad at anything arguably falling within STEM. Some drill back to their earliest memories of grade school where teachers told them they weren't skilled in an area that felt like a great source of joy or interest for them, and thereby turned them off that path, resulting in a profound loss. Fast forward thirty years, and clients have internalized the idea that they can't balance a checkbook, or apply to work at a tech company, or consider going back to school for an engineering degree, because "I'm bad at X." These internal voices can be so powerful that they've caused clients to decline opportunities that would have taken them in entirely new directions, with more money and more satisfaction, and, most importantly, that would have allowed them to share the vast resources of their internal gifts to change the world for the better.

When we fail to see these memories and experiences underpinning our limiting beliefs as systemic rather than personal, it's easy to believe that the failing is ours and that there's something wrong with us, and to internalize that belief as real. However, when we overlay the example I've given above, for instance, with the fact that STEM professions have historically excluded women and girls, and that replicating those systems by denying girls access and communicating their claimed inherent unworthiness is a form of unconscious bias that preserves the status quo, we start to see that the beliefs we've internalized as a result of our personal experiences are in fact the baggage of cultural oppression, systemic oppression, misogyny, and patriarchy, and not, I cannot emphasize this enough, *our shit to carry.*

If this feels familiar to you, I urge you to off-load that luggage by choosing to consciously name your limiting belief for what it is: internalized oppression. That's the first step to recognizing that *the problem isn't you.* It may not feel that simple to you, I know, but if you can identify any nugget of the memory you're working with that might be representative of larger systems of oppression or the maintenance of the status quo of power, you are dealing with baggage that isn't yours to carry.

And I want you, most importantly, to *give it back.* Decide right now that you're not going to carry that trash around in your own head for a minute longer, and that the next time that particular limiting belief arises, you're going to remind yourself that it's not about you, that the events that taught you that belief were attempts to imprint you into culturally indoctrinated norms, and that you will send that belief on its merry little way, right back to the nasty structural source of oppression from which it came, in favor of believing in *you* instead.

Why is this so important? Well, as I discussed in the opening of this book, internalized oppression is insidious. What we think impacts our behavior, our choices, our actions in the world. Internalized oppression keeps us from stepping fully forward to claim our gifts; from collaborating with others authentically and for change; from using our voices to shift our own lives, our work, and the world; and in the worst instances makes us agents of patriarchy and white supremacy to keep others down. It also conveniently operates to reinforce systems of oppression by working on us internally, to keep us in our designated place, without anyone having to say another word about it.

Now, here comes the good part: if you are able to recognize that the limiting belief you're working with isn't yours, but rather belongs to systemic and institutionalized oppression, do you know what that means? *It means there's nothing inherently wrong with you.*

In other words, if you consciously choose, every day and until that voice no longer has power over you, to give that baggage back to patriarchy, white supremacy, homophobia, to the source of structural oppression from which it came, *you will consciously reclaim your own worthiness. You will consciously reclaim your own power.* And almost immediately, the limits you've placed upon yourself that line up with the harm that was perpetrated against you in the past will vanish, and a whole new world will open up.

Now, I want to make one thing clear: handing your baggage back to patriarchy, as but one example, does not mean that structures of oppression instantly disappear, nor the seemingly endless ways in which those structures play upon us. But it *does* mean that the way in which we interact with those structures begins to change, first in small ways and eventually in very big ways, because we've become conscious of how we've been played. (I've got way more to say about that in the coming chapters of the book, so stay tuned.)

But let's just say hypothetically that you're sitting here reading this right now, and you've mined a memory (or just skipped over this section because your limiting belief is clawing onto its place in your head for dear life, shouting that it's true), and you're thinking, well, I kind of get it, but this particular limiting belief is *actually true, really really true,* and *you can't talk me out of it.*

Not to worry: that's where we're going next.

UNPACKING THE VOICES IN OUR HEADS: GETTING TO THE TRUTH

If you've mined the origins of a particular limiting belief or set of beliefs, and you're still convinced the limiting belief is true, you are dealing with a particularly vociferous member of your Board of Directors. This is nothing to be ashamed of. We all have them— the members of our Board of Directors who are so loud and so convincing that they're nearly impossible to dispute.

This is where truth work comes in. In order to unmask this part of your personality for what it is, I'm going to ask you now to go deeply into what that voice is saying to you, in the first person.

Here's how it works—and again, I'm going to remind you to be kind to yourself throughout this process, because frankly, most of the time, this gets pretty gross. Take a deep breath, and promise yourself that there's a reward coming at the end of this, because here's how it starts.

With your pen and paper, or on your computer, I'm going to ask you to write down every single nasty thing this member of your Board of Directors says to you, in the first person. This will pretty quickly become a list. Usually, it starts with "I'll never be able to do X because I am so awful, unworthy, unqualified, etc., etc.," and with the voice unleashed, a litany of horribleness pours out. Let it. Be honest with yourself as you do this, because hiding the ways in which we talk to ourselves allows these limiting beliefs to fester, and as the great Brené Brown points out in her work, shame can only fester in silence.

Write it all down, all of it, until you're done. Again, I've had clients write a few sentences here, and others write a dozen pages. You'll know when you're done because it will feel like you've emptied it all out.

When you're finished, take a break. A good long one—at least a day. During that time, I'm going to ask you to reward yourself for going deep into the muck. Take yourself out for a good meal, go for a walk on your favorite path in the woods or the mountains, soak in a warm bath. You've done good, hard work here, looking at the dark depths of this Board member and their messaging to you.

And then, when you're ready, a day or two later, I want you to come back to the list of statements that you wrote out so completely—because the next step of this is where the rubber meets the road.

Look at the list of statements you've written. Put yourself in the position of reading them as if you were your best friend, your most loving parent, your kindest, dear-hearted partner, and ask yourself: *Is this statement objectively true?*

Why am I asking you to do this? Because most of our limiting beliefs are objectively false.

Read that again.

It's the truth. Most of our limiting beliefs are objectively false, but confirmation bias (remember that pesky little phenomenon?) would have us believe otherwise.

Let's take an example. I had an LGBTQ+ client in her late thirties who had spent her whole adult life focused on career and very much wanted to settle down with a partner, and maybe have a kid. She'd been on a few dates since her last relationship, but hadn't found the right person, and had reached the point of believing she never would. When I asked her to do this exercise, her limiting belief statements read as follows:

"I'm never going to find my person. I might as well give up."

"The gay community in this city is so limited, and I've tried so hard already. Plus, this community is so incestuous and everywhere I turn I run into someone I've already gone out with."

"I'm too stressed all the time to focus on being open to the kind of woman I really want to be with."

"My dating history is a mess and I can't imagine anyone would want to date me given that."

"My last serious girlfriend cheated on me repeatedly and I should have seen the signs and ended things, but I didn't, and now I'm not sure I won't make the same mistake again. I'm scared I will pick someone who doesn't have their shit together."

She wrote out this and a whole lot more, and it was really hard work. She paused for a day, and took care of herself, and then returned to the work with this question for each line: *Is this statement objectively true?*

Line by line, she examined her writing, and she, like all of my clients, discovered something critical: there was a mountain of evidence disproving her limiting beliefs. She had at least five examples of women in her circle who had found long-term relationships at her age or older. New people were moving to her city all the time, and on top of that, she'd been operating in the same circles in her life for a long time, not venturing out to new places or looking around her for new potential partners she might not have considered. While her last girlfriend had been really deceptive and manipulative, she checked herself with the recognition that she was worthy of a wonderful partner to share her life with, and with a little work on her past trauma, believed she'd be capable of choosing well.

Presto: she shattered her own confirmation bias and undermined her most powerful limiting beliefs that kept her from taking brave new steps toward the truth of her own worthiness and the relationship she'd been wanting. Within a few months of doing this work, she found a new partner right under her nose in the form of a colleague from another division in her workplace. They are now married and raising a daughter together.

Critically, the process I've described in his chapter works on every limiting belief, no matter the area of your life, the belief itself, or you as an individual. Why? Because limiting beliefs, you'll recall, are absolute, and *absolutes are almost never true.* There's very little in this world that is "always" a certain way, or "never" possible. Sure, it's hard to argue with gravity, but reforming your life, your career, your community, your nation? Not so hard when you start to see that limiting beliefs *are designed to limit us, and that falsity is endemic to their operation.* When you get to the truth, you find nuance, space, and, most importantly, *opportunity,* which is what we'll get to in detail in section three of this book.

Now, I should make one thing clear in case this all sounds like magical thinking up until this point: the limiting belief you're working with won't magically disappear when you realize, through this work, that it's not shored up by the evidence. Even if you can go through your list one by one, note that each belief is false, and identify evidence to the contrary, your work isn't done. Limiting beliefs are like grooves in our thinking, worn deep and thick over time, and hard to reroute without conscious effort. Some of our limiting beliefs, in the hands of particularly vociferous Board members, refuse to let go and even fight back—you'll notice this if you catch yourself creating scenarios in your life designed to invent evidence to prove the belief. (If, for example, you're like the client I just mentioned, working with limiting beliefs about the possibility of a solid long-term relationship, a shitty date with a narcissistic person who she nonetheless sleeps with would create "evidence" for her confirmation bias to grab onto like a life raft to save her limiting belief from destruction.)

Moreover, you may come across some limiting beliefs that *do* have a bit of objective evidence to support them. If we take the example of my client, the circle in which she socialized was in fact pretty incestuous, and she was exhausted by that. What then? Well, the key here was to separate the objective fact ("the social circles in which I'm traveling are not offering me what I want right now") from the limiting belief ("I'm never going to find my person"). One may be true, but the other is not. Strategic thinking *around* the limiting belief—for example, "What might need to change to get me to where I want to go on this issue? Do I need to explore beyond my immediate circle of friends, or look for love in a different way or place?"—can open up possibility and undercut the limitation, as it did for her.

Remember when I said kindness to yourself was a part of the process here? Counteracting limiting beliefs and their effect on your actions requires consciously working on your thinking, with a hefty dose of forgiveness and patience and self-love throughout the process, and an understanding that sometimes it's two steps forward and one step back. Keep going. Progress, I will remind you, is rarely linear, and it's still progress! Heroines do not have to be perfect to be heroines.

And getting ourselves out of the grooves of our limiting beliefs requires creating new grooves to settle into. As a result, I'm going to leave you with one last arrow for your heroine's quiver on the topic of limiting beliefs: the tool of creating your own new, fastidiously amazing, beautiful, and self-honoring belief structures. In other words, the tool of mantra.

UNPACKING THE VOICES IN OUR HEADS: MANTRA

Let's say you've made your list of horrible statements that your most insidious Board member has been saying to you, and you've identified all the evidence that proves each one of those statements false. The key to really off-loading those beliefs for good is this last step along the way: creating your own new, affirming beliefs, and using them as mantra.

Those of you who have experienced meditation and yoga practice are already familiar with how mantras work. A given sound, like Om, is repeated over and over again to imprint a message, a vibration, a belief, into the person saying it. Repatterning your thinking to end limiting beliefs that have harmed you works in much the same way.

Go back and have a look at that list you've created. Look at all the evidence you've accumulated that disproves it and undermines your confirmation bias. Take a minute to recognize how profoundly hard this work has been, and give yourself a round of applause—go on, do it—for getting so deep into the muck and coming out the other side.

Now I'm going to ask you to do something beautiful: create new beliefs to replace the old ones, and to do it from a place of profound self-honoring. Again, an example:

Let's return to the executive who believes that she will never get ahead in her profession because she started late. "No one respects me at my job because I went to college later than everyone else here and got a late start in this profession," was the limiting belief that was churning in her head day and night. She's put that one on her list, and when she looked at it, she realized that she had, in fact, a lot of examples of people in her current job and in her industry who have treated her with profound respect, and even with admiration for her decision to go back to school, get her degree, and launch into her chosen profession. She now gets that her limiting belief is inherently false.

But still, late at night, when she wakes up at 3 a.m. and can't go back to sleep, the limiting belief sometimes plays its tape back to her, and even though she knows it's not true, she struggles to stop it.

It's time for her to write a new belief, a new mantra, to replace the old one.

Using positive, present-tense language, she looks objectively at her path, her choices, her career. She looks inside herself to find the truth of her gifts and what's possible for her. She writes the following: "My qualifications in this profession come from the totality of where I've been. My path is unique and makes me uniquely qualified to succeed. That I started later than others means that I bring more life experience and judgment to the table. My wisdom is an asset, and I convey that to everyone I meet."

That, my friends, is how you flip the script.

So as a final gesture toward your chosen limiting belief or Board member, I'm going to ask you now to sit down and write a new belief for every old one that you've undermined. Make it positive. Make it self-honoring. Make it true even if it feels like a stretch. Write it as if you're talking to the best part of yourself, with love and dignity and honor. If you're struggling to write it, share it with a trusted friend or partner. Ask for help to make it resonate with the truth of who you are and what you want to live into for the rest of your life.

When you've done it right, this new mantra should give you goosebumps, hit you in your solar plexus, induce a sense of light and joy and hope, because you're telling the truth about, for, and *to* yourself.

And then, if you would care to, you can go a little wild. Print out your new mantra and tack it up inside your kitchen cabinets. Write it in dry erase marker on your bathroom mirror. Tape it to your monitor at work. Tuck it into the visor of your car. Whisper it to yourself before bed and when you wake up in the morning. And most importantly, when that pesky old Board member comes calling, turn to face it in your mind's eye, and say that powerful mantra to its face.

When you change the inner, you change the outer. When you change the way you talk to yourself, you inevitably change your actions. When you change the way you engage with yourself, you change the world as well.

This is how it starts. You are worthy. You belong. You are a heroine.

Believe it, and all things are possible.

4.

Gifts

Since 2017, my company, the Gaia Project for Women's Leadership, has run an online program called RISE: An Activist/ Leader Bootcamp. In that program, we take women who are aiming to be change agents in some area of their lives through eight weeks of hardcore investigation of how they can do the work they are here to do—as women, as activists, and as leaders in their field of influence. It's not an easy process, particularly at the beginning, when we ask our participants to investigate their own limiting beliefs, and the ways in which they've held themselves back.

At the end of our first week of work in the program, when we've asked women to do the limiting belief work you've just read about, we then ask them to do something else: to identify their gifts and skills, and consider how they might apply them to change the world. What always surprises me every time is that what I expect to be hard work—the struggle to evaluate and discard limiting beliefs—is actually eclipsed by the struggle to name what we're actually good at, where we're brilliant, and how we offer inherent value to the world.

I suppose it shouldn't surprise me so much. After all, we're trained as women to be self-critical because the world is so critical of us. It's the pain of it, though, that is always so evident. When I do this work live, for instance, the reactions face-to-face are humbling. If I ask a woman in a corporate setting to say out loud what she's good at, I'm often met with nervous laughter, down-turned faces, blank stares, or actual welling up of tears. In our online program, my team is always flooded with messages about the struggle to name inherent gifts and assets, along the lines of "this is really hard," "I thought about this and had to stop because it hurt too much to think about what I've given up on or discarded," or "I just can't come up with anything here. Help!"

Just in the same way that we internalize cultural bias and personal criticism and turn them into limiting beliefs, we also internalize messaging as to the worthiness of our inherent and learned gifts, skills, and assets. If the messaging that we're given relentlessly is that we aren't worthy, gifted, skilled, or successful, speaking the ways in which we *are* all of those things becomes an act of rebellion—one that can invoke its own terror field in real time.

This manifests in large and small ways. I've worked with women, for instance, who *never* celebrate a win at work—even really big ones. Instead of celebrating success, sharing it with loved ones, allowing colleagues to shout praise, many of us will barely take a breath at a win, and simply move on to the next crisis or the next goal. But doing this undermines our self-esteem and devalues our gains from the inside out. This is one reason why I insist that my private clients celebrate every single win in their lives, even if it's just by taking a day off or soaking in a warm bath at the end of a victorious day or, better yet, by letting others plan a celebration for them. If we don't do this, we're sending the message to ourselves that our wins don't matter, that our talents are valueless, that *we* don't deserve to be celebrated.

Similarly, I've seen more women than I can count verbally downplay their achievements when congratulated on a recent success. Saying things like, "Oh, I was just in the right place at the right time," or "I'm really lucky to have the boss I have," when congratulated about a promotion, for example, sends the message to other women—and to yourself—that your success is an accident or a matter of happenstance, rather than the result of your hard work, growth, and assets. One of the hardest things to do for many of us is to simply take the compliment, say "thank you," and internalize positive feedback for what we've achieved.

In the bigger picture, I've sadly seen women abandon gifts that bring great joy to their lives. This is particularly true of women I've worked with who have a phenomenally creative talent, in music or art for instance, but who were told by parents and teachers that they could never make a living with their talent, or that their talent wasn't worth pursuing because they'd never succeed, or who were simply shamed for taking such great joy in creating. Rediscovering those talents as a force for change in the world and a source of pleasure and joy is profoundly healing work not just for us as individuals, but in the context of the difference we are here to make.

You may be wondering right now why the work of identifying and celebrating our gifts matters on the path to becoming heroines. You may even be tempted to skip this step—which, by the way, is a defense mechanism created by internalized devaluing of what we bring to the world.

Here's why identifying your gifts is so important: it's a critical offering to yourself *and to the world* to celebrate your gifts, your achievements, your success, and your work. Our gifts are here to light the path to our mission in life. And in my view, we aren't fully living into our goddess-given purpose if we do not offer our gifts back to the world in ways that make it a better place.

Taking in and sitting with your own worthiness, and the value of your gifts, leads to the ability to be able to offer those gifts back to the world in ways that create profound change for you and all those around you, that live into your mission and create a legacy to be proud of in the future. I've watched women realize that their gifts in advocating for diversity and representation didn't have to just extend to the boardroom but also could extend to making films and television, and therefore benefit millions. I've watched lawyers who specialized in real estate awaken to their true gift in fighting for migrant children, and completely change focus to become legal activists for change. I've watched artists who believed their craft was just a hobby awaken to how their work moved people, supported them, created hope and inspiration and the drive to carry on. Truly, the difference we can make by tapping into our gifts, celebrating them, and offering them back to one another is profound.

THE CHALLENGE OF IDENTIFYING YOUR GIFTS

A pause for a little bit of personal philosophy: I believe that we all come into our lives with inherent gifts. Some of us are gifted with the skill of language, others with skills of connection and relationship building, some with a facility for numbers, art, music—the list is endless. These gifts are acts of grace—favors from the universe, if you will, that light the path toward our purpose and mission in life.

As we've already discussed, we receive messages from the culture, our families, our friends, as to whether these gifts are more or less worthy (or not worthy at all), and those messages may cause us to diminish or even abandon our gifts on the assumption that they don't matter, or aren't worthwhile. Our inherent gifts never wane, however. We may put them into hibernation or cultivate them to the highest heights, but they are ours, now and forever, waiting for us to return them to the sunlight.

Here's an example from my own life: I've always been a storyteller. Even as a young child, I made up stories and, when I was able, created my own books with staples and lined paper. There are notorious stories in my family of books that I created in grade school about the experiences of children escaping from the *Titanic*, for instance.

I wrote my way through high school and college in student newspaper articles and poetry and fiction. I loved to write, and was often found in the hallway of my college dorm with yet another notebook, filling pages with journaling and poems and stories. As my activism grew, so did my writing, and I reveled in creating a weekly column in the progressive student paper that relentlessly pushed limits and advocated for social and cultural change, often by telling the stories of those who'd struggled or suffered in the absence of it.

Later, when I became a lawyer and an entrepreneur, I largely abandoned my love of storytelling—or so I thought. Then a funny thing happened: I decided to write this book. But it wasn't until my father reacted to the announcement of my book contract that I realized that my storytelling had been there, lying dormant and waiting, all along. He said to me, "You've done a lot in your life, Elizabeth, but at your core, you've always had a gift with words. You're a natural writer. This is what I've always thought you were meant to do." Sometimes we need a mirror for our gifts at a serendipitous moment—a parent, a friend, a colleague, a therapist, even a complete stranger—to see things that we have forgotten in ourselves.

At various moments in my life, if you had asked me whether I was *still* a storyteller or even a writer, I would have said, "Well, if you count the hundred-page appellate brief I just wrote, maybe. But not really. No." I would have described storytelling as something I used to do, something I'd abandoned.

I now look back and realize that my gift for writing and storytelling never really left me. Even as a lawyer, I was able to tell the story of the facts of a case both in court and in writing in ways that made me a very compelling advocate, particularly in human rights cases where justice was profoundly needed or long denied. Sure, I could do the legal analysis on precedent and I could work the legal arguments in front of a judge or jury, but my real skill was always in telling the story in ways that had an emotional and personal impact.

It wasn't until I stopped practicing law that I began to see how this gift had served me as a lawyer, would serve me as a thought leader, and would then lead me back to storytelling in writing, in the form of articles and public speaking and, finally, this book.

It's not just our inherent gifts that we might discount as our lives progress, however—it's also the skill sets we acquire as we learn and grow. We can birth and develop new skills that we then carry with us for life, though our own thinking may limit what we believe those skills can do for us. They are just as valuable on the path to becoming a heroine, and we must not neglect them nor the value they bring.

I often help clients confront their inability to recognize the value of their acquired skills when I work with women who are desperate to make a career change. Those of us who have been in a particular profession or industry for a long time may be blinded by the idea that we have no or few transferable skills, and that we'd have to start over from scratch in a new line of work. For some of us, the idea that we don't have acquired skills that we could use elsewhere prevents us from even exploring the possibility of other lines of work or other ways to use those skills for good.

A few years ago, I worked with a client who had spent her life as a marketing executive in the wellness industry. Over time, she'd become disillusioned with her work, convinced that she had in fact contributed to harming women more than helping them by trying to work within a system that insisted on oppressive standards of perfection. She felt trapped. And she'd been in the profession so long that she couldn't see how her skills in marketing, and the lessons she'd learned by observing how the wellness industry plays upon women struggling with self-esteem and body issues, could apply in any other context.

The breakthrough came when I asked her to think about the skills she'd learned by reflecting on her career—how women were hurting, self-critical, self-abusing even, and how marketing sold artificial solutions to those problems when it could be applied in other, beneficial ways instead. In a day-long session to try to get to the bottom of how her assets weren't really as limited as she thought, and after some writing and coaching to remove her blinders regarding her own gifts, she suddenly realized that she could apply her messaging skills for good, rather than to capitalize on pain. From there, it wasn't long before we were mapping out an entirely new career trajectory for her as an entrepreneur, with a business idea that catered to solutions for older women who were struggling with body positivity, creating health and wellness based in self-acceptance and radical self-love instead of self-hate.

Taking off the blinders is a key to identifying our gifts and skills so that we can use them as we're meant to use them in the world. Begin by making lists of your gifts and acquired skills, and consider how you've applied them in your life and work in the past. As you work through this, I encourage you to use your creativity in defining your gifts. Write down everything you can think of that someone, anyone, might consider to be an asset or a gift. Take off your self-censor and *just write*. If you can do this successfully, when you move on to consider how to apply your gifts going forward, you might be astonished to find that you have far more arrows in your gifts-and-skill-set quiver than you'd ever guessed.

BUT REALLY: I DON'T KNOW WHAT MY GIFTS ARE

Let's just say, hypothetically, that you find yourself at this point in the book with a serious mental block. You understand that our inherent gifts are valuable, that they point us toward our purpose in life, and that giving them back to the world is a part of the heroine's journey. You just don't know what your inherent gifts *are*.

You are not alone. Many of us are so steeped in the messages about our lack of value or inherent worth that we can't see a single gift we might have to offer. This is where our friends and loved ones can help.

More than a decade ago, I was fortunate enough to take an online business class with Marie Forleo. I was still a practicing lawyer, and I was lost. I had some business ideas that were starting to take shape, but I wasn't sure I was on the right path. What was I here to do? And could I do it?

During the course of that class, as we were considering our business plans and our marketing messages and our assets, Marie asked us to write to our friends and family with a profoundly vulnerable question: What are five things that I'm naturally good at?

I approached this exercise with absolute panic. Talk about a terror field. What if nobody answered? What if nobody had anything good to say? My response to even the thought of that exercise shook me to my core at the time, notwithstanding having what many would call a hugely successful career trajectory by external standards. I realize now that it scared me because it was *about me*, about my inherent value, and the gifts that I was born with.

I was asking my friends and family to *really see me*, and more than that, to *reflect it back*.

Nervously, I went ahead and did it anyway. It took me a few days to press send on the email, but I did it. And what came back to me rocked me to my core.

My friends and family didn't just send a few words—they sent whole *lists* of gifts and skills they saw in me. Communication. Connection. Love. Loyalty. Honor. A profound commitment to justice. A warrior spirit. A dedicated heart. A soft underbelly of generosity and kindness behind the armor I wore out into the world. An often-unnoticed wicked sense of humor. The lists went on and on and on.

I cried at my desk reading what my loved ones had written. And I'm not exaggerating when I say I was changed permanently, in drastic ways and at what felt like the cellular level, by seeing what others saw in me that I had not acknowledged in myself. I remember this moment as the moment where I knew that I had underestimated who I was, what I was meant to be doing in the world, and why, fundamentally, I was here.

So, in the spirit of paying it forward, if you are truly struggling with identifying your gifts, skills, and assets, I'm going to ask (nay, demand) that you text or email five of your closest and kindest friends and family members and ask them to respond with a list. What are you good at? What are your strongest gifts and skills? What do they see in you that you might not see in yourself?

I guarantee that it will change you to have your phone or inbox filled with the reflection of who you are in the eyes of those who love you most. It may shatter you to the core to see the ways in which you have not seen what is possible for you—all the good, all the beauty that you bring to the world for those who know you. You'll land at a place on the journey to becoming a heroine where you see and honor yourself in a new light.

And in the coming chapters, we'll use those gifts and skills to identify how you can speak truth to power, grow in community, advance and create change, and make a better world for all of us.

5.

Silencing and
Finding Your Voice

During the time that I was a practicing lawyer, I loved appearing in court. While the structures of my law firm life were profoundly oppressive and difficult in the day to day, court was another story. Examining witnesses was a blast. Creating that "gotcha" moment in cross-examination was a thrill every time. And making a deep, intellectual argument to a judge that led to a win for my client in furtherance of justice? There was nothing like it.

Unfortunately, though, I didn't always get to speak my peace in court. Time and again, I was interrupted by male lawyers, cut off, even insulted in open court. In one case, I was assigned, as a mid-level associate, to manage a portion of discovery in what was at the time the largest securities class action suit that had ever been filed in the United States. In that role, I was asked to argue a critical motion before the court on behalf of lead counsel, which comprised some of the most accomplished trial lawyers in the nation. I prepared for weeks for the hearing, even though it should have been a slam dunk for our side, memorizing key points of every relevant bit of case law. It was a pivotal moment in my career.

Fast forward to a federal courtroom in Baltimore, where dozens of counsel from both sides of the case were gathered. I rose to make my argument, taking questions from the bench and hitting key points for why we should win, with extensive notes in front of me reflecting my preparation. All of a sudden, however, I felt a hand on my shoulder. Next to me was a man, a co-counsel no less, who I'd encountered multiple times before. Short and in his sixties, he was notorious for his scorn of women attorneys, and his firm had been sued twice for sex discrimination.

Before I could turn to face him, he shoved me from the podium. Notably, this was not the first nor the last time he did this to a female colleague, suffering no professional consequences despite it. In this instance, I tried to intervene, but the court allowed him to continue, assuming that he was my supervisor on the plaintiff's side.

He then proceeded to try to make my argument for me despite the fact that he was woefully underprepared. By the end of the argument, having missed all our key points and having destroyed my case law analysis due to his lack of preparation, the court ruled from the bench for the other side. We lost a motion that we should have handily won, all because this man didn't think I was up to the job and set about silencing me, no matter the destruction to our joint clients.

This is but one example of the silencing I experienced during my days as a lawyer. On other occasions, I was told by senior male partners that I should not speak up as much in client meetings, as I would "scare" clients or "intimidate" other lawyers in the room. In annual performance reviews, I was advised to be "less ambitious," whatever that means, and to make my ambitions less known within the firm, despite the fact that younger male peers were literally going door to door in the firm asking for promotion support. Over and over again, the message I was given was that my voice was not welcome and that I'd do better to be quiet and more deferential, should I choose to even speak at all.

These experiences are not unique. Silencing is a relentless tool designed to keep us from reaching our full potential. Indeed, who among us, as women, has not experienced some version of it at one point or another in our lives? I've never encountered a single one of us who hasn't at some point been told, explicitly or implicitly, to shut up, be quiet, be more genteel, to not speak unless spoken to, to be less aggressive or assertive, to be more deferential, to laugh less, laugh quieter, to keep our opinions to ourselves—let alone been directly physically or professionally threatened for speaking out. The list of ways in which women have been and are silenced daily is truly endless.

Experiences like this lead us to doubt our own voices. After years of this in my own life, I would find myself routinely doubting my communication skills—should I offer my opinion in this meeting when I knew the partner in the room missed a key legal point, or would that be considered "too assertive"? Should I advocate to depose that CEO when I knew I could do it, or would that be perceived as "too ambitious"? Worse yet, if I was silent in a meeting or other professional event, would I then be accused of not speaking up when I should have?

I'm going to let you in on a secret when it comes to silencing and using our voices under patriarchy and in traditional masculine leadership models. The secret is this: we can't win.

We are either too assertive or not assertive enough. We are either too loud or not vocal enough. The way we laugh is either "too grating" or "too cute." We are either too ambitious or not ambitious enough. We. Can't. Win.

And to make it clear: this is by design. When we are back on our heels, worried about how our communication might be received, paranoid even as to how we sound, we're not focused on working together, changing the world, making an impact, or even doing our jobs. Silencing is designed to cause our failure. And our failure maintains the status quo.

Silencing, in other words, is a tool of oppression. And reclaiming your voice and using it for change is a key step on the journey to becoming heroines.

HOW HAVE YOU BEEN SILENCED?

Consider for a moment the evidence of silencing in your own life. When is the first time you can remember being told to be quiet, stay in your place, hold your tongue? For most of us, we were children when we first got this message. Even if we were lucky enough to have parents or teachers who encouraged us to speak our minds, it's never long before the culture steps in to correct our trajectory.

As with limiting beliefs, over time, the ways in which we've been silenced can be internalized. "My laugh is abrasive," one client told me, "so I've learned to just smile with my mouth shut when something is funny, so people don't get put off." Another client, born in China, had been told by a white male supervisor that she was hard to understand and was desperate for an "accent coach," even though neither I nor my team struggled in any way to understand her. She then cried when we put voice to how racist this treatment of her had been. Still another was afraid to speak up in school board meetings dealing with the bullying of Black children based on hairstyle in her school, for fear of being stereotyped and labeled "the angry Black lady."

I'll say it again: silencing is a tool of oppression—of systemic sexism, racism, homophobia, of verbal and actual violence designed to preserve the power of those in charge. And when silencing is internalized, it becomes self-reinforcing.

And so the question I ask clients routinely in the face of it is this: Do you believe you have the right to speak your mind?

Note that I am not asking about the *ability* to speak one's mind. I am asking specifically about the *right*. Why? Because when we realize that we have the right to speak our minds, we reclaim our own power and worthiness. When we realize we have the right to speak our minds, we start to reclaim our voices.

Notably, on the first try, the answer to the question is not often yes. I've had to coach countless women to understand that *yes*, you do have the *right* to speak your mind. Your right to free expression is actually written into the Constitution, and limited in only very rare circumstances that might incite a riot. Speaking up in a meeting or in the streets is not among those limits.

Exploring the ways in which you've been silenced, and exploring your own internal messaging about whether you have the right to speak your mind and to be heard, are critical steps on the path to uncovering and using your voice as the heroine you are meant to be.

SILENCING AND SPACE

It's important to also note here that silencing isn't always about our voices—it's also about access. There are spaces into which we are not invited. There are spaces where we are not welcome. There are spaces where our very lives are at stake should we choose to speak up. If we've been confronted with these spaces our whole lives, using our voices for change may feel terrifying, even impossible.

For this reason, when I'm working with clients to overcome silencing and toward using their voices for change, I ask them to identify where they feel safe to speak their minds, right now. For some of us, it might only be in a few tight and intimate relationships where we know we're loved, respected, and seen. For others of us, local organizations where we're active or we volunteer may provide that room. My hope is that all of us can identify a least one space, at one time in our lives, where we knew we could speak our minds and be valued for it.

The key to pushing forward through silencing and toward speaking out is to sink an anchor into the fact that our voices have mattered and do matter and will matter going forward. If we have used our voices even just once for positive change, we can do it again. Imprint what it felt like to have that experience into your bones. Breathe into that sensation. Trust that you matter, and that you are here to use your voice to make a difference.

NOT EVERYONE WILL LIKE YOU.
AND THAT'S OK

Now, here I have to let you in on a key challenge in combating silencing, and this one is personal: in a word, haters. In prior incarna-
tions of my professional life, I had haters who were men who were
in competition with me, or men who were shocked when I out-
matched them in court and set about to destroy me as a result, or
those who saw something in me that simply rubbed them the wrong
way and caused them to destructively act out. In recent pandemic
times, I've had followers become so annoyed at interruptions from
my children during Zoom calls that they've attacked me for addressing the needs of my kids, despite my pointed discussions on
the importance of being generous to those balancing parenting and
working from home at the same time. Like many women with large
online profiles, moreover, I've had haters online—including in some
instances women who have actively sought to destroy my business
and my career just because they have not liked something I've said,
leading all the way up to cyberstalking.

In almost every single instance, with rare exception, I have
taken these experiences exceedingly personally. I am a profoundly
sensitive person—which is an asset, to be sure, for coaching and
consulting, but a serious pain in the ass for a public intellectual.
There have been instances where I've felt online attacks and drag-
gings as physical harm in my body, and one instance in particular
where a series of attacks over a period of ten days felt, no exagger-
ation, like the stress of what I was experiencing might literally
kill me.

In milder instances of merely being disliked or criticized, however, I'm prone to obsessively trying to figure out how to make things right or analyzing what I might have done to provoke criticism. Despite having a loyal and loving audience of hundreds of thousands of women online, I've spent many a night poring over the comments of the one lone nasty person who doesn't like me, wondering, Why? What did I do wrong? In recent years, I have had *whole months* where I have wanted to shut down all my social media accounts, and run away once and for all from vulnerability, in favor of hiding under a blanket on my couch where no one can criticize me except my kids.

If any of this sounds remotely familiar to you, please know that you are not alone. One of the key features of patriarchal indoctrination includes the fact that historically, our ability to survive was conditioned in many instances on our ability to please and to placate men. Somewhere in our DNA—and my epigenetic DNA in particular, apparently—we learned to fear for our survival if and when our speaking out caused someone to dislike us, criticize us, or reject us. At other times—and for some of us to this day—using our voices has posed a threat to our very lives.

I want to make clear here that I am not and would never advocate for anyone to use their voice for change in instances where they are under threat of physical harm or death without consciously choosing to do so. For some of the bravest among us, that threat is a part of how we choose to make our greatest impact. However, in many instances in our daily lives, we as women remain silent because we've been taught to be afraid of the response, even when the consequences aren't a matter of life or death, or even dire. We choose to stay silent because *someone might not like us*. And that, my friends, is tragic.

In one instance not so long ago when I was struggling with a vociferous bout of criticism, a long-time activist said to me: "Listen, Elizabeth. If you're here to make a difference and here to create change, you're going to have to face the fact that you *will* be hated. People are not going to like what you say. People are not going to like what you do. *You can't create change and keep people comfortable at the same time.*"

This aspect of reclaiming one's voice is a path many of us will walk for a lifetime. While my own comfort level with using my voice for change has increased exponentially over time, and while my tolerance for others' discomfort with it continues to grow, I'm certain that in my own case I'll continue to be challenged by it along the path. In each and every instance, however, I come back to what another dear friend said to me years ago when I was confronted by yet another man who found my voice too "intimidating":

"What other people think of you is none of your business. Keep going."

MAKING SPACE FOR YOUR OWN VOICE

In the next chapter, we're going to spend some time talking about what it means to speak truth to power in real, concrete terms, and how to speak out to be heard, communicate effectively, and create change. Before we get there, though, I want you to think about one more key feature regarding using your voice for change, and it is this: *Where* can you most effectively use your voice for change right now?

I believe that at this moment in history, there is no place whatsoever where the voices of empowered, awake women are wasted. Are you in a corporate environment with a major pay disparity? Use your voice for change there. People may not like it. Keep going. Are you in an industry dominated by "manels"—panels made up exclusively of men, and usually white men at that—at every industry conference? Use your voice for change there. People may not like it. Keep going. Are you upset at the imbalance in housework or child care in your own home? Use your voice for change there. People may not like it. Keep going. Are you profoundly angry about the actions our government has taken against immigrants, voting rights, progressive policies? Use your voice for change there. People may not like it. Keep going.

Identifying where you can make the greatest impact is one of the most important steps to becoming a heroine, and *every place you do it* makes a difference. Consider it a pebble, or a boulder, thrown into the lake of change. Every ripple makes an impact. Every ripple changes not just what's on the surface, but everything that's underneath.

Shirley Chisholm, the first Black woman elected to Congress, once famously said: "If they don't give you a seat at the table, bring a folding chair." Make your space. Use your voice. Get ready, because what comes next is a major step on the path to creating the change in your life, your work, and in the world that you and I both know we all need.

People may not like it. Fuck 'em. Keep going.

6.

Starting to Speak Truth to Power

At this stage in our journey, we're ready to start taking steps forward in new ways to create change. We've examined and begun dismantling the imprinted beliefs and structures that have held us back, and continue to work on reprogramming the messages that we've been living with for life. We've evaluated our gifts, and how and where we might best use them. And we've considered how we've been silenced, and how that's impacted our communication for ourselves, for others, and in the world.

Now, we reach the point of reclaiming courage, and beginning to speak truth to power.

My own story on speaking truth to power began in small stages, and it began as a means to process and overcome trauma that I'd been carrying around for years. As you'll learn in the later chapters of this book, I was repeatedly molested as a tween and teenager by a family friend who was also, in all sorts of boundary violating ways, a family therapist to me and others in my family unit. It took me decades to talk about the harm he perpetrated on me in public settings. The shame I had related to this experience, and particularly to the response of certain of my own family members to it, silenced me for longer than I care to remember.

In 2015, however, something changed. I attended an event in Seattle called Urban Campfire, run by the indomitable Melody Biringer, where in a room of hundreds of strangers, women got up on stage and told the true stories of their struggles and their passage through their own journeys. As I sat in that room, I realized that not only was it possible to tell the stories of our trauma without shame, but that it was healing to ourselves *and to others* to speak these stories out loud. Moreover, speaking them out loud was a way of disabling their power over us, and therefore disabling the power of oppressors to silence and control us going forward.

A few weeks later, as fate would have it, Melody invited me to tell my own story to a smaller room of participants in a more intimate event. I accepted. On a cold night, in the Greenlake area of Seattle and with a few close friends in the room, for the first time, in public, out loud, and to strangers, I told the story of my molestation and how it broke my family apart. I left no detail untouched. And I watched as others cried and grieved on my behalf, remarked on my strength and bravery, and asked me to share more of how I'd grown from trauma into thriving along the way.

That event was terrifying, but it also felt like a big exhale. Once I'd shared the story in public that first time, doing it again became less frightening. Doing it again, in fact, started to become a tool for change, liberation, and revolution.

Fast forward to the end of 2017, and the breaking of the #MeToo movement. A dear friend of mine, Connie Vasquez, who is also a survivor of child sexual abuse, organized a rally in New York City to speak truth to power in a much larger way. That day, in a blizzard and in front of Trump International right next to Central Park, I ascended a platform with a microphone and a big PA system and major national and international media coverage, and I told my story again. This time, though, there were hundreds in front of me on the street, strangers walking by, television cameras rolling, and wide exposure everywhere. This time, my story wasn't just for me and a small room—it was a story about victims everywhere being seen, heard, valued, and understood. I ended that speech knowing that my voice was a powerful force for change, that the story of my abuse was a part of what had made me who I am now even though I wouldn't wish it on my worst enemy, and that I had built my courage into a force that could lift not just me out of grief and shame and rage, but others as well.

Since that event, I've had dozens of women approach me and tell me they watched the speech online or in person, and that it changed them—that it empowered them to tell their own stories, to find greater courage, and to move toward using their shame as a transformative force for change by speaking what they previously thought would have to remain secret forever. One woman wrote to me and told me that, despite being in her late sixties, she'd never had the courage to tell anyone what a male relative had done to her as a child until she'd heard me tell my story, and that, as a result, she was finally beginning to heal. Another told me that as a rape victim herself, she'd been compelled to begin to work to address a backlog of rape kits in her local area that had prevented access to justice for victims.

This is an important reminder: when we share our stories, we create ripples in others that carry out far beyond our immediate imaginations and circles. When we lift our voices, and bear witness to others as they do the same, we are all changed.

VULNERABILITY AND VOICE

In the last chapter, I asked you to consider in your life where you have felt safe to speak your mind. For some of us, that may be a tiny space—for instance, in conversation with our best friend, or in our most intimate relationship. For others of us, we've cultivated communities where we can speak our minds freely, even if we don't feel free to do so out there in the world.

Right now, I'm going to ask you to imagine what it would be like to speak truth to those in your life or in the world who really need to hear it. Imagine what it would feel like to say what you want to say, what you know needs to be said, to those who have held you back—or better yet, to those who might be able to collaborate with you to help you create change. Imagine saying all of that in a way where it is actually heard.

What would it feel like, in your body, to do that? What are the emotions, sensations, responses you'd have to speaking those truths out loud? How would that experience change you, perhaps for the rest of your life? Give yourself permission to feel every feeling that comes up as you consider this.

Your initial reaction to even thinking of this might be one of abject terror. I know that response, because I've been there. But remember the terror field? It applies here, too. Keep going.

Courage and bravery are always required whenever we are considering speaking truth to power. Sitting in discomfort is a skill set that applies here in full force. We must feel the fear and do it anyway.

I can tell you from personal experience that speaking truth to power is like building a muscle. Starting with small stretches prepares you for more heavy lifting. But don't diminish what those initial stages will do to change your life. Mine shifted dramatically in the space of a few months when I decided to start speaking out, and healed so much shame I'd carried around for so long faster than I ever could have imagined.

A BRIEF WORD ON SAFETY

In examining how and where we start to speak truth and tell our stories, it's important to recognize that *where* we choose to use our voices is a matter of privilege. For some of us, public spaces are safer than they are for others. The operation of systemic oppression means that certain circumstances, as well, carry with them inherent risk for some but not for all. Consider, for example, what it means to be a white man asking a police officer why he's been pulled over without cause, versus a Black man in the same circumstances. I myself once talked back to a police officer who had blocked the road to my kids' school after he yelled at me to move my car. It wasn't until a few minutes later that I realized my privilege allowed me to do that without ever once, in the instant of deciding to yell back, considering that he might shoot me for doing it.

Without question, the safety (or lack thereof) in speaking truth to power is in every circumstance inflected by institutional, systemic, and interpersonal oppression. The environments in which we speak up are more or less safe depending on who we are, where we are, and the visibility of our diversities. Some of us may realize that we choose to remain silent because the very real fear for our safety has been ingrained by the harm our culture has perpetrated on us again and again. For others, this observation may be a wake-up call that not all of us are safe all the time, or in all circumstances.

As a result, the first question I always want to ask in discussing strategies for beginning to tell our stories and communicating truth to power is whether your safety—physical, emotional, financial—would be put in danger by doing so. As with all risk, safety tolerance varies wildly from person to person. I've worked with people who have faced down police in riot gear and guns as a part of their activism, and kept going. I've also worked with single mothers who have decided that their health insurance and job security mattered more than taking up a battle against their employer on every single issue for fear of retaliation, and with a decision to move on to a better place as soon as possible. Each of us must evaluate what safety means to us, and how that applies to every circumstance within our own lives as we seek to step into our heroism.

As well, it's important to think about how we can create safety for others who might not have the same privileges that we do. We're going to talk about allyship and listening and creating safe space as we continue through this book, but for the time being, I'll just say this: if you are not working collectively with others to create greater safety for all of us to speak truth to power and create change, you're not doing enough.

For now, however, I encourage you to consider where and how you feel safe using your voice, and whether there are circumstances where you've used your voice (or not) in spaces where you've felt unsafe. What is your personal tolerance for safety when it comes to effecting change? Recognize that your risk tolerance is inflected by your background, the culture in which you live, and all forms of oppression. Understand, as well, that you have more or less safety depending on your privilege. If your privilege guarantees your safety in circumstances where it doesn't for others, is safety a crutch for you? Further, how can you collaborate with others and ask for buy-in to create safety for yourself and others?

In this regard, it is critical to differentiate between situations where we feel unsafe for fear of being judged for speaking up—spaces where we may need to stretch to grow—and those where we are facing down true harm, where systemic oppression and violence could put us at real risk. Understand that a part of leveraging privilege for change is speaking up when and where others cannot *even when it's uncomfortable*, using that space to educate, organize, and mobilize to the benefit of ourselves and others, creating room for historically silenced voices to be heard, and also knowing when to shut up and listen, which we'll discuss later on in the book.

Throughout this work, I ask you to forgive yourself when past concerns about others' judgment or your own shame might have stopped you from speaking up. Recognize that this, too, is inflected by cultural oppression, and is a prime target for change.

That said, discomfort is a part of change, and pushing yourself toward courage within the bounds of safety is mandatory to this work. Every step along the way will require you to stretch in the direction of your freedom and that of others. Without your bravery on your own behalf and as an ally, nothing changes. We'll work more on how to create that as we proceed.

COMMUNICATING WITH SKILL AND VALUE

Speaking truth to power doesn't just require finding the right environment to explore the vulnerability of speaking truth, and making sure you're safe. It also requires the skills to communicate in a way that can be heard and understood, and that furthers difficult conversations. A key to this is understanding and applying strategies of Nonviolent Communication (NVC), a methodology founded by Marshall Rosenberg. Nonviolent Communication invites us to speak from a place of our own values, and to communicate (and listen) from a values-based perspective. On the next page is a graphic that summarizes the strategies of NVC.

When I discuss NVC in corporate training programs, I always suggest that the first and biggest takeaway from NVC for me has been the use of "I" language.

By way of example, there was a senior partner at one of my law firms who would tear down the hallway late at night when he was displeased with the work of an associate, shouting, "You really screwed that up! You'll never make it as a lawyer if you don't fix your brief writing!"

Notice here the difference in how it feels to be the colleague on

How You Can Use the NVC Process

Clearly expressing how **I am** without blaming or criticizing	Empathically receiving how **you are** without hearing blame or criticism

OBSERVATIONS

1. What I observe *(see, hear, remember, imagine, free from my evaluations)* that does or does not contribute to my well-being:

   "When I (see, hear) . . . "

1. What you observe *(see, hear, remember, imagine, free from your evaluations)* that does or does not contribute to your well-being:

   "When you see/hear . . . "
   (Sometimes unspoken when offering empathy)

FEELINGS

2. How I feel *(emotion or sensation rather than thought)* in relation to what I observe:

   "I feel . . . "

2. How you feel *(emotion or sensation rather than thought)* in relation to what you observe:

   "You feel . . ."

NEEDS

3. What I need or value *(rather than a preference, or a specific action)* that causes my feelings:

   " . . . because I need/value . . . "

3. What you need or value *(rather than a preference, or a specific action)* that causes your feelings:

   " . . . because you need/value . . ."

Clearly requesting that which would enrich **my** life without demanding	Empathically receiving that which would enrich **your** life without hearing any demand

REQUESTS

4. The concrete actions I would like taken:

   "Would you be willing to . . . ?"

4. The concrete actions you would like taken:

   "Would you like . . . ?"
   (Sometimes unspoken when offering empathy)

the receiving end of "you really screwed that up," as opposed to "when I got your brief, I was surprised to see that you didn't delve more deeply into X issue." One puts the other person immediately on the defensive, and produces a fight, flight, or freeze response. The other is an expression of ownership of the response. Stages one and two of the NVC approach create openings for discussion on difficult topics in particular.

Stage three is critical because it is a statement of the speaker's values. Using our example above, consider the impact of a statement that goes like this: "When I got your brief, I was surprised to see that you didn't delve more deeply into X issue. One of the things that really matters to me is making sure we're thorough in our work product."

The key here is that it's hard to argue with a statement of values as long as those values are in integrity. Obviously, valuing discriminatory impact (more on that later) is not a value in alignment with becoming a heroine. However, values like openness, transparency, clarity, connection, and growth create opportunities even when topics might be stressful.

Lastly, stage four of NVC is an invitation to buy in to further conversation. Again, using our current example, consider this approach: "When I got your brief, I was surprised to see that you didn't delve more deeply into X issue. One of the things that really matters to me is making sure we're thorough in our work product. Could you explain to me your thinking around this issue?" Again, the NVC approach builds connection and conversation to reach an amenable conclusion, without creating defensiveness in the other party.

Similarly, NVC can be used to de-escalate conflict. Consider, for example, the boss that comes screaming down the hallway with "You really screwed this up! It's so late!" or worse. Applying NVC principles, a de-escalating response would go like this: "I can see that you're really upset that I turned in this project after the deadline. What I'm hearing is that you value promptness. Would you be open to discussing how this happened, so I can be sure to meet your expectations going forward?" Again, the recognition of the other person, their response, their values, and a request for buy-in conveys immediately that you are willing to engage in conversation to reach a solution, rather than fight back in a defensive manner.

I am not suggesting that any of this is easy in real time. NVC takes practice—to the point where, when I review these principles with corporate clients, I often suggest they find ways to practice NVC daily, so it becomes a habit rather than just a tool to be rolled out at high-stress moments. Moreover, it helps to apply it not just in work environments, but also across all aspects of your life. It works remarkably well with children. It works well in most marriages, assuming that there's no ongoing anger management concerns or abuse present.

Most importantly, however, it works in high-stakes conversations on power and oppression. I've coached high-profile women of color on how to use NVC to discuss race and gender bias in hiring and termination decisions so that the impact they're seeing to the detriment of equity is put on the table for clear discussion. I've worked with the parents of trans kids on how to apply these principles to strive for gender nonconformity training in their kids' schools. By communicating observations and the need for change from a values-based perspective, awakenings in those who have never considered the impact of their actions or policies become possible.

Now, a word of caution: unconscious bias inflects everything, and as with any aspect of communication, if you are not aware of your own internalized biases and have not worked to dismantle them, NVC will reflect those biases. A classic example of this is the statement "we just hire the best person for the job." This past year, I learned of a truly disturbing situation where the CEO of an investment bank, when asked about the lack of diversity in hiring, simply responded with that statement.

Note that "we just hire the best person for the job" might sound like a statement of value, in line with NVC principles. However, in reality, it's a statement of unconscious bias. It says to the person asking the question: there aren't enough people who look or love like you, or with your abilities, that are good enough for this job. It also fails to reflect the speaker's own responsibility for the lack of diversity and equity in his own company, let alone respond to the origins of it through real and systematic policy change.

Other examples of statements of purported value I've seen that are actually evidence of bias include childless supervisors stating a value of round-the-clock availability to employees with young children, or stating a value for in-person work when a colleague is caring for a sick parent at home. The labor of caregiving falls more often than not to women, and imposing value without understanding that can result in explicit acts of discrimination.

It's critical that recognition, as a stage on the heroine's journey, includes reckoning with our own internal programming. This is a constant path of self-reflection we're walking, including as we move from recognition into the work of reconciliation. In every way that we communicate, including and most importantly as we begin speaking the truth of our stories and the truth of our lives, we must consciously work to dismantle the ways in which structures of oppression demand that we internalize and repeat their messaging. Look around, particularly, at who you're talking to and who you're listening to. Wherever you are privileged, are you working to listen to those who are not? Are you advocating for those less privileged than you and creating space for those voices to be heard? Are you accountable to others as well as yourself? Notably, reconciliation, where we're heading next, requires reconciling with our own programming, as well as with others.

Practice NVC in your life with conscious consideration for what you might have missed and what might still be left to learn. Do your best to receive constructive criticism from a place of receptivity and connection, rather than fragility or defensiveness, to continue your trajectory of growth. And remember that perfectionism is a tool of oppression, and learning to use your voice for change carries with it inherent risk. You *will* mess up at some point. You'll offend someone, your unconscious bias will bleed through from a place you haven't yet examined, and you'll have to choose how to incorporate the lessons that come with that. The question is whether you will choose to learn and keep going, or recede into silence (or sometimes recede, learn, and then keep going). I urge you to choose to keep going, with kindness to yourself, listening to others, in integrity with what you value most, and with the understanding that every step along the path to becoming the heroine you are meant to be will include periods of needing to stretch your voice and your vision in uncomfortable ways for the greater good.

In other words, you have to keep carrying the vessel even

though it has holes in it, because what leaks out creates growth. Keep going. You've got this. Yes, you do.

PRACTICAL SPACES FOR CHANGE

Lastly, it's worth considering in real time *constructive locations* to start flexing the muscle of speaking truth. Particularly, I invite the women I work with to evaluate in real, honest terms the relationships and spaces where they know they can expand their voices to create greater impact toward a better world.

Could you be saying more in your workplace about the conditions and environment in which you work, and how it could shift to be more inclusive? Does the school your children attend or the local Democratic party need a greater awareness that you might be able to provide on a key issue? Have you witnessed discrimination in public places where you know you need to shout it out? What nags at you, when you consider this question, as a place that demands your voice?

As mentioned earlier, I started telling intimate stories and making big-picture demands for change in small groups where I knew I was protected. Over time, the rooms became larger and larger, as did the audiences. Each step along the way required more courage, and also, concomitantly, an evaluation of what I needed to feel safe as balanced against the demand for my voice and the impact it could have on a wider scale.

Now I routinely tell my stories and advocate for change on stages in front of tens of thousands live and online. That does not mean it's always comfortable and it does not mean I never fuck up.

But it does mean that with every expansion of my courage and my bravery, and through a commitment to constant self-reflection and listening, the impact of my voice for the greater good expands as well. This, too, is confronting the terror field and beginning to find ways to speak truth to power to create change.

And it's worth noting that you don't have to become a compelling public speaker, or even leave your house, to be able to make a massive impact by using your voice. One of my favorite stories on evaluating practical spaces for change came from a client who was essentially housebound due to a disability. Nonetheless, she decided that if she couldn't leave her home, others would have to come to her. She now routinely hosts postcard-writing parties on behalf of candidates she cares about, first in person and then on Zoom during the pandemic, and tens of thousands of those postcards have landed in voters' mailboxes thanks to her efforts.

A key recognition on the path to becoming a heroine is this: *our voices create change.* That includes yours. You, too, have the capacity to make a difference. One person can change her life, her community, her nation, and the world for the better. Every action you take to lift your voice and the voices of those who have been marginalized and silenced creates space for all of us to be valued, for all of us to be loved, for the world as we know it to shift in favor of all instead of a few.

However you can use your voice, do that. Do more of that. Start today.

You're planting seeds for the future in the ashes of what came before, and that's the first step toward real change.

Section Two
Reconciliation

7.

Trauma

’ve lived through a lot in my life. For a long time, I believed that the traumas I’d experienced (and, let’s be real, continue to experience) had fundamentally damaged me and that there was no getting back to who I might have been absent intervening events. As a tween and teen, I was molested repeatedly by a family therapist who was also a friend of my parents. For years, it was hard for me to speak to all but a handful of people about what had happened to me. I worried about what others would think of me if they knew I had been molested, or that my mother had abandoned me in favor of aligning with the man who molested me, or that I’d been involved with someone throughout my twenties who abused me in violent ways that left scars on my body, while justifying his own misogyny by claiming that I wanted to be treated that way. For a while, I tried to claim the mantle of being damaged as a point of pride, hoping that it would ease the burden of judgment I was placing on myself and that others placed upon me as well. At one point, a family member said to me that I should just stop talking about being molested to others within the family, because if one in four women were assaulted before adulthood, and they managed to continue on in silence, I should be able to do the same.

I believed that if people knew what had happened to me, they'd want nothing to do with me, and further, I believed that the harm done to me had erased my value and rendered me fundamentally worthless. I believed that I was unlovable, incapable of a healthy relationship, unworthy of motherhood even, and that I would never return to that "pure" state before all that trauma.

These abject fears governed my days for longer than I care to admit. It wasn't until I was thirty-two and began a relationship with a slightly younger, wildly embodied and patient man steeped in kindness and generosity and willing to listen to every part of my story that things began to shift. One night, in particular, after finally sharing the worst of it, and after hours of talking in his tiny apartment in Queens, he looked across the bed at me and said, "You know, Elizabeth, there's nothing wrong with you." It was shattering. He saw me through a lens through which I hadn't viewed myself, and it changed everything. He was a mirror of reflection back at me, made possible only by my own vulnerability and my willingness to reckon in real time and with another human being with what I'd lived through, no matter how much it scared me.

I start here, at the entry point for reconciliation, because reconciliation begins with reconciling with ourselves first, and with the kindness to ourselves that was offered to me in the experience

I described above. We are merciless and terrible in the way we treat ourselves with regard to the traumas we've lived through. And if we do not reckon with the damage we do to ourselves in the wake of trauma, if we cannot find compassion for ourselves for what we've lived through and what was done to us through no fault of our own, we will be unable to reconcile external oppression *without re-creating it at the same time.*

Do you find yourself sitting in judgment of your own experiences and your own worthiness, as I did? Do you play the "trauma olympics" by either assuming your trauma is worse than that of others or by looking at the trauma of others and thinking "at least I didn't have it that bad, why am I so depressed?" Have you blamed others for what they've experienced as a part of not confronting your own trauma? Faulted others for being mistreated in similar ways? Trauma manifests in multitudes, and while your shame may be internally directed or externally directed at others in the form of projection, it's there, unresolved and unwitnessed, unconsciously playing out across your life.

Why is it so important to call it out? Because shaming others or yourself for inflicted trauma is the replication of patriarchy and structures of oppression. When we tell ourselves, or others, that we are less-than because of what has been done to us—spiritually, emotionally, physically—and when we allow those stories to impact our self-esteem and our sense of our own worthiness, we are inherently doing the work of domination for the structures that perpetrate it.

So we start here, with how we reckon with our own trauma, and how we shame and berate and silence ourselves with it, how we tell ourselves these stories that we are worthless and forever damaged and that no one will love us because we've lived through horrible things, because this is what systemic oppression wants us to believe. It's such a convenient narrative, isn't it? The longer we believe that we are damaged and to blame, and the more we tell others that they are damaged and to blame, the easier it is on those in and with power to continue perpetrating harm for the sake of it.

If we return for a moment to the myth of the Daughters of Danaus, and consider ourselves as that filter through which life-giving flows, we must also ask ourselves what we need to filter *out*. There is garbage we retain, the heavy metals of trauma and the mud of our messy experiences that, if not cleared out from time to time, will stop the flow that we need for rebirth. We must clarify what we are carrying within, digest the pain, integrate the lessons, and allow the trauma to be released, so that we are not impeded on the path toward growth.

To that end, I'm here to tell you a few things that you may need to hear:

- You were born inherently good and worthy
- Those qualities have never left you, and cannot be taken from you by anyone or anything you've experienced
- No matter what you've been told, you belong here
- You are perfectly imperfect, exactly as you are
- You are not your trauma
- You did not deserve it, you did not cause it, you did not invite it, and there is nothing you could have done differently to change it
- You matter

- While your experiences may have marked you—physically, emotionally, spiritually—you are in charge of how and whether you integrate them into your life
- Your healing is within your control, even though the journey may be lifelong
- You are lovable, beautiful, and inherently valuable
- What has been handed to you through trauma is a function of power, and it can be handed back to where it came from
- You are enough, you are seen, and you are loved
- You are stunning in your survival, your strength, your choice to continue on your path, and your will to rise
- None of what I've written here is a lie
- And the same is true for all of us

I'm going to let you in on a secret: there is not a single woman I've met in my life, let alone among those who I would deem to be heroines, who has not at some point faced down some absolutely horrible shit, things that are unspeakable, so heavy with the weight of carrying them that we feel they might break us forever—until, one day, they don't.

GETTING GROUNDED IN WHAT'S YOURS AND WHAT IS NOT

I'm often asked about what I "did" to heal from the traumatic experiences of my childhood and early adulthood. I'm not going to lie: that healing is ongoing, and it will be until the end of my days. As with the never-ending spiral of the heroine's journey, there is a never-ending sense of peeling back the layers of trauma. Just when you think you're done, there's more.

That is not to say that it's a hopeless endeavor—in fact, quite far from it. There are instances, to be sure, where it's taken me years or decades to off-load trauma in a way that feels like it doesn't irrationally impact my behavior or my thoughts from time to time. I've touched upon almost every viable trauma modality out there as I've worked to process my experiences—from psychotherapy and Western medicine, to family systems work and counseling, to various forms of body work to address trauma held in my body, to energetics like Reiki and cranio-sacral work, to soul retrieval, past-life regression, quantum healing, and other forms of spiritual work, across a wide range of belief systems and methodologies. Nothing I'm suggesting here should be a substitute for doing that work, or pursuing any methodology that calls to you as being necessary or relevant on your own path.

All that said, a turning point in my own work came when I began to process my trauma through the lens of power. Because here's the thing: *intentionally* perpetrated trauma is *always* experienced through the prism of oppression.

And if it is, then the unpacking of trauma, the reconciliation with it, must always include an understanding of how power caused it, how power engendered it, and how power continues to want you silenced and ashamed.

As with your limiting beliefs, this baggage that you carry *is not yours*, never belonged to you, and isn't a permanent accessory to your trajectory. You can—and I would argue, to create change, *you must*—give it back.

Some of this sits in your own consciousness, because once we wake to the fact that there is no intentional trauma that isn't also about structures of power and oppression, that violence can't exist outside of it, it's impossible to ignore any longer the fact that what you've lived through is not inherent to your character, to your person, or to your soul.

So how do we go about giving back the trauma that was perpetrated upon us? We start by speaking it, over and over again, in spaces of safety, as we discussed in the last chapter. Integrating our traumatic experiences, and handing back what does not belong to us, can only happen if we are able to speak out loud what has been done to us in the name of power.

And as we've already discussed, choosing safe spaces in which to begin telling your stories and to begin processing your trauma is a key to moving through the experience of it.

Sometimes, though, the safest space is with yourself. And that's where we're headed next.

PURGING WHAT HURTS

It may be that for you the idea of telling anyone, even the most trusted person in your life, the story of what you've experienced is too terrifying to consider. I've worked with women who have lived through profoundly abusive bosses, violence, sexual assaults, who carry with them a deep imprint of shame, who have been in need of a way to begin the process of healing by confronting it privately. For example, a client of mine had been through an incredibly painful divorce in her small town, where her ex-husband spiraled into mental illness, sometimes manifesting in public events that were disturbing and violent. Embarrassed and ashamed of the far-worse private events that led her, finally, to leave him, but knowing that she needed to begin to process what she had lived through, she wasn't yet ready to speak with anyone close to the situation about the facts of what she had experienced. Instead, she needed to clear her own shame first in order to proceed. We worked through the exercises I am about to share with you as a part of that process.

While I am all in favor of seeking out support whenever you know you need it—and indeed encourage you to seek mental health care whenever necessary along your path—if you find yourself in a place where you are afraid to speak the story of what has happened to you to another person, I'm going to invite you to begin the work of healing by getting your trauma out of your body first.

What do I mean by that? I mean that you should write it down.

Clear yourself some space—physical space, yes, but also some time when you won't be disturbed. Choose one traumatic experience, and write down every aspect that you can remember from it that feels relevant, as you did with origin work in prior chapters. Write it as a stream of consciousness, and write until you're done. Again, you'll know when you're done because it will feel as if you have emptied it all out—all the muck, all the garbage, all the hurt—and put down everything that needs to be said.

To get there may take you fifteen minutes or several sessions over several days. That's OK. Do it for as long as it takes to describe that one experience. Once you're done, though, I'm going to ask you to do something radical: I'm going to ask you to sign what you've written with a statement of gratitude.

Why would I do such a thing?! you may be thinking. Here's

why: because we are breaking cycles. Because we are ending what hurts. Because we are integrating what we've learned. Because the lessons are real.

A statement of gratitude can be quite simple—something along the lines of "I am grateful for the lessons learned. I am complete with this now," followed by your signature. Or, you may wish to list all the takeaways from a given experience. I have found it helpful to write down, for instance, something along the lines of "I never have to experience this again."

Do what resonates for you.

Then, take a break for a day or two, and do something kind for yourself: sleep late, play with a pet, snuggle your partner or your kids. Get grounded in the now, as opposed to the past.

And then, after a bit of a break, we get to the really fun part: working with the elements to commit to the processing of trauma and its return to that from whence it came.

I encourage you to print out what you've written or tear the pages from your journal. Then, take a breath, and set them on fire.

Yes, literally set them on fire.

I have a particular fireproof vase that I use for this purpose on the regular. Fireplaces are good for this, too. So are pots on the stove under a range fan if you live in an apartment. But whatever your safe and secure choice, burn that trauma up. Turn it into ashes. Let it go.

And when that's done, I'm going to ask you to commit the ashes of your trauma to either the earth or the wind. When I lived in New York City, I would regularly open a window at the end of this ritual and send the ashes of what I'd written flying on the wind out over the Hudson River. Alternatively, now that I have a garden, I have buried those ashes in the dirt as fertilization for new growth. Choose what feels right for you. You may choose a place that has some significance to you to release the ashes, or you may choose a windy peak that will allow you to watch them disappear on the wind.

After another day or so, I want you to sit down to write again. This time, I'm going to ask you to write down what you are welcoming into the space within you that held your trauma instead of what you've now released. Maybe you're welcoming in kindness to yourself. Maybe it's support and love from your community. Maybe it's awareness of your gifts so that you can give back to others. Maybe it's a beautiful new job where all your talents are appreciated and well-compensated. Write it out. Let it flow.

And then, you guessed it, I'm going to ask you to commit what you've written to another element with which we have already become familiar: water. Again, when I lived in New York, I would write down my welcome messages on biodegradable paper, gather up some flowers, and commit the writing and the offering to the estuary of the Hudson River. I've also done this ritual on the coast of Costa Rica under the full moon, wading all the way into the Atlantic Ocean to call in what I wanted. I did it once in a river that ran through a forest in Jamaica on New Year's Day with a few friends.

Make what you're calling in light or make it deep, but make it known: you're ready to step into the flow of something more, and you're committed to it. Trauma has been transmuted and has paved the way to something new.

One last thought here: this may sound facile to you, too easy, unworkable. It may sound like something a bunch of naked Wiccans might do in the woods. That's OK. Do it anyway. So many clients—*so* many—have begun this process with a healthy dose of real-world skepticism, only to find themselves immeasurably lightened by the end of it, astonished by the gravity of the shift.

Why? Because we carry with us the skills of our ancestors, buried long and deep within us—gifts of the women who came before us, those magic-makers and spell-casters and healers of children and families and nations, though we may not know their names or their exact methods. When we wake to the rituals that connect us to things bigger than ourselves, the context of how power has silenced us and kept us small becomes apparent, and we get to start doing the real work we came here to do.

So go for it, even if it feels a little silly. Set your skepticism aside for a moment, and be willing to feel something far older than yourself. Pay attention to how you feel on the other side of it.

Just as the earth beneath your feet holds the compost of all that came before, the blood that flows through your body holds the tales of your ancestors. They're here, too, living on through you, and their magic works.

A BRIEF WORD ON TRAUMA, RAGE, AND OVERWHELMING EMOTION

Early in 2020, I had the opportunity to interview Dr. Shaili Jain, a trauma researcher and post-traumatic stress expert at Stanford University. Dr. Jain had recently written a new book entitled *The Unspeakable Mind: Stories of Trauma and Healing from the Frontlines of PTSD Science*. Although I chose to interview her for our year-long online program entitled Healing the Heroine, at the end of the interview I turned off the record button and just began to talk.

As one does when one has lived through trauma and finds oneself suddenly in a safe space, my stories of trauma poured out of me. Dr. Jain and I barely knew each other, even though our work is related, but there were things I realized in my interview with her that had never been explained to me before by any clinician or healer I'd worked with.

The dominant one, the one that shook me to my core, was that uncontrollable rage was often a sign of unresolved trauma.

I'd come into the most recent chapter of my work at a pivotal point in my career and life. My marriage had ended due in large part to violent outbursts by my ex-husband that had, I now realize, remapped my brain for hypervigilance and amplified trauma from earlier in my life. Then, shortly after the 2016 election, and as you'll learn in later chapters of this book, a series of events online led to the near-destruction of my business, threatened my ability to provide for my children, and kicked up another round of abject terror. Lastly, there was the day-to-day trauma that was triggered by living during the Trump administration—the constant onslaught of violence, gaslighting and disinformation, misogyny, injustice—that was layered on everything I'd experienced in the past, amplifying it to a dangerous degree.

It led me to a place where the tiniest bit of negative criticism or lack of control over my immediate circumstances sent me into uncontrollable rage.

Underneath that rage, though, was profound, abject terror.

In the era in which we live, there is healthy rage, and then there is unhealthy rage. There is a natural drive toward defending ourselves, and then there is unhealthy hypervigilance.

Beyond that is the origin of epigenetic trauma—an area of science that is only now being explored—where the trauma we experience is mapped onto our DNA and passed down through generations. Intergenerational trauma, where our unresolved wounds are passed down to our children through our parenting and the experiences we carry with us culturally, emotionally, and through ongoing systemic oppression, is one result. In my own matrilineal line, for instance, we have a long history of women who have abandoned their daughters physically or emotionally, and there is no question in my mind that the impact of that trauma lives in my immediate family story. The grief of that is often covered up in rage, and the deep work I've had to do on that continues.

You've heard me say before in this book that when we change the inner, we change the outer. Necessarily, when we examine the ways in which trauma has altered our thinking (and perhaps, through epigenetics, our DNA), we discover the ways in which it has also altered our conduct. The ability to heal, reconcile, and integrate our own trauma is a necessary first step to reconciling our own biases and also our own relationship to power.

Again, on the path of the heroine, the work of healing trauma is lifelong. It is an alchemical process that takes time. And it's also worth noting that unresolved trauma makes us even more vulnerable to systemic abuses of power than we might otherwise believe. Trauma is what disinformation plays upon. Trauma creates openings for unconscious and conscious biases to take root and replicate. Trauma incapacitates us, even when it's most necessary that we use our voices for change. Trauma is *designed* to keep us from rising up, from overthrowing dominant power structures, by working on us *from the inside out*. And uncontrolled rage, when perpetrated on others, causes additional harm.

It's incredibly important that we remove ourselves from the role in the equation that systemic oppression has set for us. Ask yourself: What happens if I set aside my rage? What happens if I confront my grief and my terror? What's underneath that? How can I compost it into something better? What processes that underlie it do I need to look at? Who have I harmed and how can I rectify that? (More on that last one coming up.)

Keep asking yourself these important questions, and remember: we are not after perfection. We are after consciousness, and the capacity to make better choices. Integrate the rage, transmute the fear, and you will land in a place of clarity that will shift how you walk in the world, and what good you can do.

And if from time to time you feel stuck, if a blind spot is presented to you or you discover a place within yourself that isn't yet excavated or that you've ignored, the good news is that the work of healing that issue can start at any time, and can always begin again. Commit to your own work. Do it now. If entire worlds live within us, then truly working to heal ourselves is a starting point for healing everything that is broken in our world.

And as I learned throughout my journey thus far, in the words of the great Leonard Cohen, "There is a crack, a crack in everything. That's how the light gets in."*

*Leonard Cohen, "Anthem," track 5 of *The Future*, November 24, 1992, Columbia audio.

GETTING GROUNDED
IN INTEGRATION

Not all that long ago, it was unfathomable to me that the traumatic experiences of my early life would ever reach a place where they no longer caused me unrelenting pain. Over time, though, the impact of those experiences transmuted into something else. The integration of those experiences into who I am, that alchemical process of transformation, awareness, acceptance of the lessons, and continuing to walk the path, had eventually erased the pain.

For me, continuing to ask the questions I've outlined above has led me to a place of being able to state that I was hurt very, very deeply by the experiences I've lived through, and that hurt is real and true. Furthermore, what was done to me was a form of systemic violence that is condoned and excused relentlessly in our culture. It was not about me. It was done to me, but it is not mine. Instead, all that rage and grief and loss and fear has coalesced into something so much bigger than I am: an overwhelming calling to overhaul every system that caused it, so that what happened to me does not continue to happen to others.

My trauma, in other words, and the unpacking of it that continues to this day, has transformed me into a force to be reckoned with, forevermore.

I wouldn't be who I am today had I not gone deep into how I was marked by power, used and cut and harmed and abused by power, had I not done that work. I wouldn't be able to lead through it, to speak to the hurt and the change required to return to our gifts, to write it without shame and speak it without fear, and, most importantly, to cycle back from the journey to share the lessons I've learned, had I not committed to that work for good.

When you arrive at this place, your trauma becomes a teacher. Through the lens of power, and removed from shame, it offers you a path forward to aid others, change systems, propel the integration you're creating within yourself forward into action. As you continue to work through your own trauma, you will find more and more opportunities to work through the realignment of power in your own life and in the world. You will become attuned to the invitation to use what you've learned in your daily life. You'll take with you the bravery you've acquired in looking at your own experiences with a critical eye as you use your voice to reconcile with trauma in the world.

The earth beneath your feet is full of lessons, composted ashes of all that came before. You stand on the foundation of all your experiences and on the shoulders of all those heroines who preceded you, even those who you cannot name. Your obligation is to take the strength of your own survival, and the legacy that they have left for all of us, and use it to change the world.

8.

Diversity, Division, and Intersectionality

Now is a good time, if you've never done it, to consider how diversity lives in you. Reminder: diversity goes way beyond race, gender, sexual orientation. Where were you born? What was your family makeup? What was your educational experience? Was your family working-class? What generation were you born into? What about your current age? Your current financial picture? Your political beliefs? Your nationality, by birth and/or adopted country? Your primary language? Within each of us lie multitudes, a diverse set of identities that intersect in every individual.

The concept of intersectionality was first introduced by Professor Kimberlé Crenshaw in 1989, in a published paper titled "Demarginalizing the Intersection of Race and Sex." In that paper, Crenshaw pointed at the specific ways that the identities of Black women intersected in the experiences of discrimination and marginalization under the law. Though the term has been widely used and applied in other circumstances since, at its root, intersectionality points to the unique experiences of Black women in the face of systemic oppression on the basis of race, gender, and class. Moreover, understanding intersectionality in practice requires us to account for more than one form of oppression when we're considering how to dismantle systemic and institutional oppression.

Now, a word of warning: this chapter may feel a bit remedial for those of us who have a deep, personal understanding of intersectionality and oppression. Those of us who are historically marginalized, particularly in layered ways, may have a profound understanding of power and oppression in daily life, and a deep understanding of how intersectional identities can place us at the point of the spear of systemic harm. Please feel free to skim this material if that's the case. If you are a white woman, however, I urge you to process the upcoming material carefully, as your lived experiences, particularly of power and oppression, will be very different from those of Black and Indigenous women and other women of color, and perhaps in need of further excavation in terms of how white women benefit from systemic oppression while also being targets of patriarchy.

Furthermore, if you have a college degree, you come from wealth, or you were raised middle- or upper-class, your daily life and experiences will be wildly different from those with a high school diploma or less who were raised in poverty. The same is true for invisible diversities. For instance, I have a friend who is long partnered with a woman who teaches on equity and inclusion. Her conservative style of dress and her choices in appearance present as straight. Those she teaches are often shocked to learn that she is not. Similarly, neurodiverse individuals may not appear as such. Those with learning disabilities may also show no outward signs of disability.

Your identity may also include your life circumstances. I am a single mother, sole provider and sole caregiver to two young children. While this wasn't always the case, my worldview and my choices have been markedly impacted by these facts over the last five years. I've experienced harassment on the basis of my single motherhood—"no wonder you're a single mom" is a favorite line of attack from right-wing online trolls—and the professional and personal choices that I make put my children first in every circumstance. My identity as a single mom was not one I planned for, but it has impacted my experiences in unique ways, and changed me for the better as an advocate.

In addition to race, class, gender identity, orientation, ability status, marital status, immigration status, religion, parenting/caregiver status, wealth, neurodivergence or lack thereof, and education, your identity may also be tied to where you were born and where you've lived.

The key point to observe, however, is that the privileges attached to certain aspects of these identities and not others have formed a systemic hierarchy of bias. Indeed, as the brilliant Isabel Wilkerson points out in her stunning book *Caste*, the myth of race fundamentally created a caste system in America. When we start to realize that race is merely a way of categorizing worthiness and value based on appearance, the concept of race itself, and the myths attendant to it, sound insane.

We've all been indoctrinated with the ways in which our privileges—race, class, gender, orientation, and so many others—live or do not live within us. Where we have privilege, we have had attendant, undeserved, and unearned favor granted to us. Where we do not, we have struggled to see those who do achieve, succeed, and gain access to power where we have been denied. Understanding how these identities intersect is a key tool to growing our awareness, our advocacy, our compassion, and a better future.

Consider this critical exercise: make a list of every part of your identity, from the smallest features like your hair color, to more middle of the road qualities like your education status, to the widest identity you claim, like your generation or your nationality. Include everything we've discussed so far here. Once you've completed that list, review it with a critical eye. Which aspects of your identity are viewed with favor by the dominant culture? Which are not? Which ones have granted you access to places where others might have been denied? Which identities have been the basis of discrimination you've experienced? Which have not?

Understanding how privilege lives in us, and the intersectionality of our experiences that results from privilege or lack thereof, leads us to a greater understanding of others. When we can see how power has divided us, split us into tiny fractals of the totality of who we are and worked against us or for us on those bases, when we are able to understand the gravity of that impact or benefit on the story of our lives, we can also begin to understand how those who have differing identities have experienced power differently.

Furthermore, the differences that live within our identities and experiences are assets, and failing to have as much difference represented in the halls of power replicates harm. I've consulted

and spoken inside big tech companies, for instance, where found-
ers never considered how the technology they'd built could be
weaponized against women or people of color, because they had
no women or people of color on their design teams. I've spoken at
The 3% Conference, created by my friend Kat Gordon to combat discrimination in the advertising industry, and heard tell of
overtly racist advertising disasters that would never have been
greenlit had Black talent been in the room. Even in more traditional sectors like banking or law, I've had conversations with senior executives who simply didn't recognize that they were losing
business because their entirely white male teams weren't appealing
to diverse clients running businesses designed to meet the needs of
folx who aren't white and male.

Inclusion is the principle that diversity alone is not enough and
must include the fair and respectful treatment of all in our society,
and equal opportunities to achieve. Inclusion in turn is not enough
absent equity—equity in pay, equity in access, equity in power. Any
one without the other is insufficient to combat systemic oppression at work, at home, in social programs and benefits, in education, in medicine—in every sector as well as in the world at large.

Reconciling with artificial, discriminatory hierarchies and
with systems of oppression can feel like enormous, overwhelming
work. The damage we've experienced, benefited from, or perpetrated amounts to centuries of ongoing harm. The ongoing trauma
is ever present and the solutions may sometimes seem out of reach.

The key, however, is to keep digging. As we'll discuss further
in this section, continuing to peel back the layers of the ways in
which systems of oppression work on and in and through us is
a mandatory part of the heroine's journey. Every aspect of what

we reject and throw off makes room for fertile growth. Every change in our thinking and, most significantly, in our behavior, plants seeds for the future. The more we get grounded in a different way of thinking, the more we unpack the lessons we've learned and rectify the harm we've caused, the greater chance we create for revolution in our culture and society that creates freedom and justice for everyone.

BUILDING COMPASSION

Later on in this section, we're going to talk about difficult conversations and active listening, and why bearing witness to the experiences of others, and particularly following the lead of the most marginalized, is a key to change. First, though, we must cultivate within ourselves the skills of compassion and empathy.

Now, I want to be clear: I am not talking about compassion for those who wish to harm us. I grant no compassion for neo-Nazis or militia members seeking to murder people, for instance. I grant no compassion for misogynists, transphobes, homophobes, xenophobes, or those who traffic in hate of any kind. I also grant no compassion to those who enable any of the above, or sit silently by and allow those people to harm others when they have the power to stop it. Those folks have to do their own work, and it is not our job to do it for them. And calling on those who have experienced hate, discrimination, or violence to do the emotional labor of those who have perpetrated it is, in a word, bullshit.

No, when I talk about creating compassion, I'm talking about creating compassion for those with whom we are in coalition, those whose intersectionality differs from ours but with whom we may share similar aims, or those whom we know we must center upon. Compassion for others as we listen and learn, and compassion for ourselves in the experience of listening and growing, are key components to valuing difference and traveling toward one another as allies.

When you are challenged to consider the motivations of someone else, particularly someone who you know to be on the right side of history, I'd ask you particularly if you can find empathy *first*. What must it be like to walk in that person's shoes? If you don't know, it's time to build relationships where you can *ask, listen, and learn.*

I'm lucky that I have intentionally cultivated relationships with folx across every spectrum of diversity in my life. If I'm called upon to choose between hanging out with the white and white-adjacent wealthy straight moms in my community, or the wildly diverse others upon whom our communities rarely center, I'm always choosing the latter. Apart from the fact that diverse experiences and friends and relationships make life more interesting, it's also a really key way to check yourself on where your privilege lies and to constantly be growing your worldview—more on that later in this section.

For now, though, I'd like you to take a look at every place in which you operate on a regular basis—your family, your friends, your community, perhaps your kids' school, your religious organization or your spiritual practice, your political communities, and beyond. Particularly if you are white, straight and/or cisgender, look at what surrounds you. Have you unconsciously only chosen communities that look and love like you? What do you think that means for your broader approach to society at large, to equity and justice, to being an agent of change? How can you make wider

choices in your engagement that will build broader understanding? How can you grow in your compassion and understanding
for others and for yourself?

I'm going to ask you to commit to doing one new thing—maybe
something as big as joining Showing Up for Racial Justice (SURJ)
or another allies group if you are white, supporting a LGBTQ+
group if you are straight, or maybe something as small as having
coffee with someone new whose intersectionality and diversity
differs from yours—to push your comfort zone toward more of a
growth and empathic mindset. Ask yourself where privilege lives
in you. How can you expand beyond that by building wider communities? Start now.

BREAKING THROUGH

Here's one of the reasons why reconciling with intersectionality
and inequity is so important: division and disparity are tools for
white supremacist patriarchy. When we are separated, hierarchized, and divided, we are necessarily not working together toward justice and change.

An example of the radical possibility of another way of being
was presented to me during the summer of 2019. I was in the middle of organizing a mass mobilization against human detention
camps under the Trump regime, an effort that eventually resulted
in protests in over eight hundred cities worldwide. As a part of
that effort, I got a call from a pastor with a major nationwide organization mobilizing through Black churches for justice.

I got on the phone with her expecting to talk about immigration rights, and particularly how Black activists had been working

on immigration justice for decades, with the hope of further coalition building. Though I certainly had some familiarity with the organization of which she was a part, I didn't know that this conversation would be a game changer for me, and far broader than what I'd expected.

After exchanging pleasantries, the conversation veered off in a surprising direction. She told me that leaders of her organization had been considering for some time what it would mean to build a "breakthrough movement," namely a movement where every progressive organization and folks of every intersectional identity who had been historically marginalized and their allies were to come together at once to push for massive societal change. In the somewhat siloed world of activism in which I'd long operated, I'd moved from cause to cause, alliance to alliance, and issue to issue in my own organizing efforts. What I'd never considered before then was what it would mean to have true representation in a breakthrough activist movement, led by and centered on those who had experienced the most persecution and who would benefit most greatly from revolutionary change.

It was a conversation that radically shifted my view of what was possible. We've seen some of that type of movement already in the organizing leading up to the 2020 election, particularly from coalitions built and led by Black, brown, and Indigenous women. We've also seen some of this in the diverse representation visible in Black Lives Matter protests following George Floyd's murder. Examples of inclusive movements—organizing that builds upon the value of our intersectional experiences and that leads the way with compassion and, dare I say it, love—are here already. The question that remains is how we can create them everywhere, at once, in coalition.

The starting point is in our daily lives and in our interpersonal relationships. How can we unearth connection in diversity? How can we throw open the doors and undermine privilege where we have it, and claim it where we've been marginalized and denied, so that all of us have a seat at the table? Coalition, connection, compassion in diversity, valuing all our intersectional experiences and identities is the key.

Let the seeds of these ideas germinate in you. Water them with your actions. Cultivate diversity and inclusion in your daily choices by consciously advocating for it and growing it in relationship. Consider in every space you occupy who is already within it and who is missing, and work for greater inclusivity at every table at which you sit. Expand the authors and the media sources you consume to include historically marginalized voices. Ask for the opinions of those who don't hold your privileges wherever possible, with the understanding that no one diversity is a monolith of thought. Listen. Educate yourself continuously to foster your own growth. Aim always to walk arm in arm with others across the spectrum of humanity.

Please note, however, that everything in our society is built to stop this collaborative work in community. Whole systems exist to prevent it, and we're ingrained from an early age with biases that work on us to keep us separate and therefore down. As you'll see in the next chapter, the place to start combatting ideologies and systems that stand in the way of revolutionary change, that prevent true compassion and understanding and an end to hierarchized systems of oppression, is within ourselves.

9.

Attacking
Internalized Bias

I f you are a political junkie in the way that I am, you will remember the Democratic debate that took place on the night of
February 19, 2020. It was the night we saw that Elizabeth Warren, in addition to her competence and her plans and her incredible and powerful staff, also had the stiletto of accountability in
her back pocket. No other candidate left the stage unscathed,
and she was utterly brilliant and precise in showing us what she
could do.

What fascinated me in the aftermath, though, were the knee-
jerk comments from a few women in the activist circles in which
I travel that expressed discomfort: "she's too angry," "that was
below the belt," "she's nasty." I watched some of these women
engage with friends online using words like "we are women of
distinction" and "we need to show others how to be nice." While
these were a small fraction of the totality of responses I read, they

roiled my stomach. They were, in a word, an obvious manifesta-
tion of internalized bias.

Worse yet, pointing that out produced incredible defensiveness in response. Women, and arguably progressive women in
particular, don't like to believe that we carry with us internal
biases that wreak havoc on women's success. Moreover, white
women don't like to examine the ways in which, even if we believe
ourselves to be "woke," we still participate and are complicit in
white supremacy.

By this point in the book, it should be obvious that the culture
in which we live leaves marks on all our psyches. The experience
of living within power structures that are built on violence, separation, and hatred impacts us in both conscious and unconscious
ways. White supremacist patriarchy is dependent, however, on
the enforcement of its rules from the inside out. In other words,
what we wreak upon ourselves, and what we wreak upon other
silenced and marginalized people, are mandatory components of
why it continues to exist.

And education is not enough. While the work of Ijeoma Oluo,
Dr. Ibram X. Kendi, Isabel Wilkerson, Angela Davis, Frederick
Joseph, Tiffany Jewell, Heather McGhee, Rachel Ricketts, and
many others are critical reading, from whom I urge you to learn if
you have not already done so, white supremacist patriarchy has
done its work on your mind as well as your body for your entire
life. Unlearning its enforcement and your own complicity is profound and necessary and never-ending work.

The reason why this internal work is so critical is because internalized bias, when left unremedied, does an enormous amount
of damage. Internalized racism, particularly in white women, is

an endless source of harm to Black people, and it is my view that it is the obligation of every white woman to do the work of dismantling how white supremacy lives within her.

Moreover, all women must dismantle how we tear one another down, particularly as we are granted proximity to masculine models of leadership. Take, for example, any traditional corporate work environment, or for that matter, most tech bro start-ups. Inevitably within the ranks you will find a woman or two who have "made it" to the top. If you're me, however, and you're brought in to consult on the culture of the company and how its leadership could shift toward inclusivity and the retention of diverse talent, you'll hear whispers before too long about those few women at the top—and more often than not, that *one* woman at the top—who has gained access to the highest halls of power within that institution.

And what you will hear, inevitably, are horror stories from the diverse talent below those women in the organization. The female boss who insisted her female assistant complete an assignment while in labor at the hospital. The female supervisor who told her female subordinates that they needed to wear skirts, not pants, and grow their hair long, or the men in the office would not take them seriously. The white female supervisor who reported her Black team member's natural hairstyle to HR as "unprofessional," while allowing a white male team member to walk around the office in his socks on a daily basis. Stories like this pour forth on how those purportedly glass-ceiling breaking women seal up that hole behind them and are harder on other women than some men in similar positions, and are notoriously untrustworthy; how careers have been undermined, support promised and then withheld, or worse yet snatched away at the brink of a raise or a promotion; how men have been elevated easily while her own female team members have been left to flounder; and how every woman below her in the chain of command has felt it. In one health-care company for which I taught a women's leadership seminar, the most senior woman leader's presence in the room created such fear that not a single woman participant was willing to voice any professional concern for fear of retribution. Faced with silence, I learned only after the workshop, when a few women crept up and told me privately, why the workshop had fallen so utterly flat.

Now, talk to that archetypal senior woman herself, and what you will often find is that she identifies as a feminist, a glass-ceiling shatterer, and more than anything an exceptional talent. She had to be tough coming up the chain of command, she was routinely hazed if not sexually harassed, and she had to adopt certain qualities of steeliness, lack of empathy, even dissociation, to survive and keep going. Somewhere along the way, a man or group of men decided that she had shown the exact combination of skills and willingness to bend to demand that should make her one of the tiny few granted access to the halls of power, and she's worn that mantle with pride—it's made the scars of the experience justifiable, because she made it there when other women did not—because white supremacist patriarchy deemed her worthy. What she may not have noticed, however, is that this narrative of exceptionalism—that somehow she and she alone had the qualities, skills, smarts necessary to get to where she is—is now a weapon she's internalized against other women and is expected to wield against other women, without even realizing that it's there.

When I speak to rooms full of women inside environments like this, inevitably a young woman executive asks me what to do about the older women in the chain of command who are relentlessly demanding, if not cruel, to women on their teams as compared with men. "Why is she so hard on us?" "I thought older men would be the only problem, but she makes it *worse*." "She can't be trusted, and that means I have no women to mentor me." "Doesn't she *see what she's doing*?"

Unfortunately, she does not. And the wake-up call that goes along with recognizing internalized bias is often one of the most challenging and uncomfortable points of transformation we will ever confront along the path of becoming heroines—because, heads up, that woman in the front office is not alone.

Every single one of us has blind spots that have been created by the culture in which we live, and left unexamined, those blind spots become reinforcing mechanisms of dominant power structures against others. Perhaps we believe that because things have been so hard on us as we have struggled to prove our worthiness, we must be hard on others in return. Perhaps we don't consciously consider how we can uplift and empower those who have been historically silenced in our organization or in the world. Perhaps we respond defensively when called to account for the privileges we hold in the spaces in our lives, rather than listening and considering how we can leverage and undermine our privileges to the benefit of those who have been denied them. The examples are endless and the work of unraveling them is lifelong, but the key is to start, and to keep going.

HOW DO I RECOGNIZE
MY OWN BIAS?

For about four years early in my legal career, I worked at a law firm that was on the cutting edge of human rights litigation worldwide. The managing partner was a boundary breaker who liked to push the limits of the law. He gave me an enormous amount of responsibility over several high-profile cases, including the management of other associates more junior than I.

One of those junior associates was a young woman just out of law school who was profoundly competitive with everyone she met. She pushed back against my oversight at every opportunity, questioned my judgment, and seemed to go out of her way to badmouth other female associates. On one occasion, she sat in a meeting with a senior partner and blamed a deadline she had blown for her own work on my failure to manage her properly.

At the time, and in the middle of this meeting, I remember consciously having to choose to control my anger. I didn't understand her desire to tear other women down. Worse yet, I was concerned about my own immediate response to her actions in that moment, which candidly approached the place of "that's it, I will do everything I can to destroy you, how dare you" sort of thinking.

I didn't end up going there. I let it slide. I stayed silent, hoped the senior partner would see through it (he did), and assumed that she would reap what she was sowing with that kind of behavior. Lo and behold, I was eventually proven right.

However, this incident, and several others like it, caused me over the course of my legal career to consider in depth the phenomenon of women constantly working to tear one another down, including my own periodic impulses in that direction. Again, this is a place where we have to look at this pattern through the lens of systemic and institutional oppression.

This firm, too, had only one woman on the management committee, and she was in the role of managing staffing, HR notably being a slot to which senior women are often relegated. Throughout my time there, junior and mid-level women were given the message, both explicitly and implicitly, that there was only room for so many of us at the top—that our success was dependent upon meeting the standards for the tiny slice of the partnership pie that was available to anyone who was not white, straight, or male. For one of us to win, another had to lose, and that meant we were more competitive with one another than we were with our often less qualified, less able male colleagues.

It's important to point out that the message that only so many of us can make it to the top *is a lie*. There's no reason, for example, why Ruth Bader Ginsburg's famous statement that there would be enough women on the Supreme Court "when there are nine" should be shocking. For centuries, our institutions have been run almost exclusively by white, straight, able-bodied men. For what reason should our institutions not be helmed by women, people of color, LGBTQ+ individuals, those who are differently abled? There isn't one.

So if we start with the premise that the idea that only so many of us can succeed is a lie, and yet we continue to compete with one another nonstop instead of banding together, we need to pose a really important question that I often find myself asking when confronting institutional oppression: Who benefits from this? Who benefits when we don't work together? Who benefits if we're engaged in constantly battling each other and tearing each other down?

Power benefits. Oppression benefits. Institutions invested in maintaining the status quo benefit. When we are engaged in competing with one another and tearing one another down, we are doing the work of patriarchy for it.

Similarly, we must monitor our own thoughts relentlessly, to make certain that we are working to counteract the biases that we've been taught. That includes internalized biases about ourselves, our worthiness, our belonging, as well as biases against others. It is profoundly important that we consciously work to recognize and undermine where bias lives in us, so that we do not replicate it, and so that we do not self-harm.

Note that this isn't just true at work. When we attack the body of a celebrity or public figure online, oppression benefits. When we critique the voice or appearance of another woman instead of her words or actions, oppression benefits. When we worry that the woman below us is trying to take our job instead of supporting her rise, oppression benefits.

We need to flip the script on this, in our own minds and in public and professional forums. We need to begin to understand that, contrary to what we've been taught, when one of us wins, we all rise. Particularly, because of the nature of intersectional oppression, when Black women win, we all rise. The more we can band together, celebrate one another's successes, and work to uplift the most marginalized among us, the more we all will gain.

It is critically important that we are vigilant in all that we do professionally to undermine unconscious bias in action, and that we understand that none of us are free from it. That said, I am often asked about underperformers or those who are engaged in abusive behavior. Let me be clear: I am not suggesting that those who choose to not meet their job requirements, when those requirements are established equitably and when conscious choices and actions are undertaken to eliminate bias in their institutions, should be given a pass. Indeed, I've coached a number of team leaders through devastating choices to terminate younger women who they adored, or hoped would succeed, sometimes those who they'd mentored and advised, but who nonetheless kept failing to meet deadlines or respond to client concerns, or who were abusive to staff or coworkers. True, we did our absolute best to make sure that in those instances every standard applied to make the decision to terminate was not inflected by any unconscious bias. Did the employee have child-care concerns that were making her late? Did she have a sick parent or spouse? Was something else going on for her professionally or personally that was impacting her performance? Was there anything the institution or the leader could do to support her growth? Was her team viewing her behavior through the lens of any unconscious bias? Also a key question: Would a man be terminated for the same conduct?

Key to choices such as these is consciousness and decision making. Go deep into your self-investigation when confronted with the impulse to critique, harm, or undermine the success of another woman, asking yourself particularly about your own motivations and underlying beliefs. Check yourself, routinely. Hold those who are engaged in any form of conscious or unconscious bias to account, with zero tolerance for those who perpetuate patriarchy or white supremacy, including when you see it in yourself. Stand in your own integrity. Be aware of stereotypes that might exist in your own mind, and of your thoughts if and when those stereotypes present, so that you can check yourself. Understand where privilege lives in you, and seek to leverage it on behalf of those who are more marginalized, and to undermine it in favor of equity wherever you can, rather than wielding it as a weapon.

There is plenty of room for all of us, and we must seek to create that space in everything we do on behalf of all those who have been pushed down or aside by systemic and institutionalized bias. Moreover, in the event that you are ever called to account for your own bias, or called on a blind spot of which you weren't aware, your responsibility is to respond with accountability, self-awareness, and active listening—more on that in the next few chapters.

Consider the work of undermining your own unconscious biases as the work of composting your old thinking for future growth. Again, the garbage we throw off, refuse to carry, recognize as not our own but something acquired from what we've been taught, becomes fertilizer for better ways of being, stronger allyship, and future building that is more equitable for all.

Throw off your trash thinking and transmute it into growth. Don't stop. The years of internalized bias that live within us must be consciously undermined on a daily basis. The process is lifelong.

RECLAIMING YOUR TIME

Lastly, make sure you're not turning your internalized bias on yourself. Just as I did for fifteen years as a lawyer in response to the wild critiques I was given about my ambition and my communication, you may have internalized comments about your voice, your smarts, your appearance, your ambition, your skill set, your gifts that flat-out don't ring true. In turn, that internalized bias may have caused you to silence yourself, to avoid applying for jobs that might have stretched you even if you weren't sure if you were totally qualified, or to not fight for more money or more responsibility when you knew it was due.

This is where, in the cyclical nature of our learning, you may have to return to the limiting belief work of earlier chapters and continue to question what is true and what isn't. Think through the messages you're telling yourself and where they come from. Ask yourself: Who benefits when I treat myself like this, when I deny the world my gifts or I turn away from something that feels right? Allow your thinking to propel your actions.

Plant the seeds, apply the compost of your old failures, and prepare for growth.

10.

Difficult Conversations and Active Listening

Early in 2018, in a late-night musing on Facebook, I asked what we should do about Trump supporters in the event that they woke up from their propaganda-laden endorsement of his leadership. It was a poorly worded post, to be sure, centering on the perspective of those emerging from under his sway, and not well thought out. Within a few days, however, it exploded into something far more significant.

In responses to that post, it was pointed out to me that my comments could be read as furthering white supremacy by centering on those perpetrating harm, rather than on those who were experiencing it at the hands of Trump and his supporters. Moreover, a number of Black women, having raised concerns in the past about whether my platform was truly welcoming to women of color, pointed out that this was not the first time my lack of awareness had been on display.

I did not respond well to this publicly. I pointed to my activist history. I had tearful conversations with two Black colleagues where I centered on my own feelings. I deleted some comments that I felt were abusive or destructive to my business. A couple of days went by where I tried to respond and navigate well, and uniformly failed to listen and to internalize the feedback that I was being given.

Finally, when several white women made announcements online that they were going to destroy my business because they felt my responses had been inadequate, and infiltrated a webinar I was teaching, I made a critically important choice: I hired a crisis manager/lawyer, a Black woman, to help me navigate, learn, and process what was happening—and also, it should be said, to make sure that my client relationships were protected from the particular attacks of these four white women while also holding me accountable to Black women in every way necessary. She was not cheap, and she was not easy on me, and she was worth every penny.

This online event continued for almost two weeks. As I tried to reckon with my own blind spots, I also found myself backed up against a mountain of unresolved trauma around security, and raising my children as a single mom with no support. At one moment, fear of losing my business and the ability to provide for my children was so extreme that I had a panic attack in the middle of the night where I thought I was dying. It was a terrifying moment of reckoning. Call it peak white fragility or a profoundly centering response, but it was an alarm bell that would not stop ringing—until, that is, I confronted my own needed work and the harm that I had caused.

The morning after the panic attack, I was walking down the street in my neighborhood, broken, afraid, and wondering how to address this circumstance head-on to be on the right side of justice and history and all the critical values that I have always tried to live by. As I returned to my home, mulling it over and over, I cornered myself on the issue of impact versus intent, and how my intent didn't matter if the impact of my words had been harmful. I decided, in that moment, to accept the invitation to investigate my own internalized racism, to shatter the myth of the "good white woman" that I had been living into, to get humble and acknowledge that I had work to do, and to proceed with the knowledge that there was no way out but through the hard reality of my own unconscious bias and the damage to which it had led.

Whole books have been written about white women, white fragility, and shame, and how our fragility when accused of racism is an enabling and complicit force for white supremacy. We run. We hide. We perform. We point to our intent. We demand "cookies" for the crumbs we dole out that don't lead to real equity. We evade responsibility. We ignore. And more than anything else, we don't listen. We focus on ourselves instead of really hearing and internalizing the experiences of Black, brown, and Indigenous people. We decline to listen and learn, uplift, and amplify the voices of those who can lead us to a better world, and from there, to become allies and co-conspirators for justice, instead of witting or unwitting participants in systemic oppression.

When I chose to really engage with how I had hurt Black women in my own community, I began by listening. I read through every comment to my Facebook post. I apologized, publicly and more than once, for that harm and for my inadequate response in the aftermath. I reached out to two of the Black women who had led the conversation, apologized, and asked what I could do to repair the injury. I took steps to do that. I listened some more.

As a result of this series of events, I then decided to embark on something of a listening tour. I attended Black Women's Roundtable in Washington, DC, an annual event hosted by the National Coalition on Black Civic Participation, where, as the only white woman in a room of more than three hundred of the nation's most powerful Black women activists, I listened and learned for several days about the challenges they were working to address. I engaged in conversation with BWR's leadership, used my platform to uplift their work, and canvassed with them through House and Senate offices on Capitol Hill on issues critical to Black women. Following this event, I was inspired and called to coalition build with some of the powerful Black organizers I met there—relationships that have now grown into a fundamental part of my role as an activist working in coalition with Black women organizers on issues of racial justice.

I kept going. One by one, I reached out to my friends and colleagues of color and asked if I needed to do any repair work with them individually. I asked how I could be a better ally. One of my dearest friends, a Black woman executive in advertising, cautioned me to continue to remember that white saviorism was a part of white supremacy, and also reminded me that while I couldn't solve every world problem, and I wasn't responsible for everyone's individual baggage, I could start with myself and continue to follow the lead of Black women. I started attending online webinars and joining groups led by Black women where issues of race, equity, and accountability were primary topics. I read as many books as I could find on race, anti-racism, Black womanism, and the exclusionary history of white feminism in political movements. I consciously built alliances with Black women in my field, and sent them work that I might have accepted previously, knowing that they were more qualified to handle it than I.

I kept going. Over several months, my company engaged in a wholesale review of our programming to evaluate how unconscious bias might be living in our work. We edited and revised our programming, marketing, and teaching for inclusion and accessibility. We reviewed our own internal policies, and also pulled in more and more Black women speakers and consultants on all topics for our live events. I personally continued to question, learn, and grow throughout this, all the while trying to hold myself and my team relentlessly accountable.

The Black women who I count as friends and allies, and the allegiances we have built as activists and colleagues, are among the most valuable relationships of my life—both those preceding this incident, and since. I have learned more from these women—particularly on advocacy, organizing, and mobilizing for change—than from any other teachers I've had, full stop. It is impossible for me to look back on this particular experience of being called to account, hard lessons included, with anything other than immense gratitude for the chance it offered me to grow and learn and become more equitable and inclusive in practice and in life.

That is not to say that I have become magically perfect on all of this. The learning curve of my own unconscious bias and my own privilege has been steep and messy. Several times since, I have harmed someone through ignorance or lack of understanding, and felt the wave of shame of my own fragility. I have also learned, however, that the antidote to the white fragility that enables and tacitly endorses white supremacy is full-throated accountability, humility, and bravery. It costs nothing to apologize, own your mistakes, reconcile to the extent it is welcomed, and commit to being better, so long as you actually live into that and do your best to keep your promises. It may feel massive at the time, but, honestly, it's the least we white women can do (more on that in later chapters), and the ongoing commitment to the work and to do no harm is where the real challenge lies.

One other note to this that feels important: white fragility is dangerous to all of us. If you are a white person who is challenged to investigate your own actions or beliefs on race, I urge you to not respond defensively, but to listen, hold space, internalize the critiques you are offered, and do your own work to become anti-racist, on your own time and without prevailing upon the emotional labor of Black women. White fragility permits the denial of complicity that led to Trump. It allows bad actors to manipulate and abuse a nation because of unredressed bias. And on a personal level, it stops us from being allies in change that could lead to freedom for all.

It is imperative that all of us with privilege of any kind confront how that privilege lives in us, and that we get comfortable with being uncomfortable in the investigation of it. Those of us who are white also need to get used to the regular examination of our internalized racism and engage in difficult conversations that lead to growth and change.

THE PRACTICE OF DISCOMFORT

Difficult conversations are uncomfortable. Conversations where we are called upon to be vulnerable, to examine our own failures and complicity, to listen to others describe how we have harmed them, are far from easy. But we don't learn inside our comfort zones. We learn from stretching beyond them.

And stretching beyond our comfort zones, particularly those involving shame, unconscious bias, or harm we've caused, may make us want to run. Staying present nonetheless requires effort.

Getting comfortable in discomfort is a practice. And as with any practice, consistency is key.

Recently, I was involved in an activist group where the leader engaged in conversations that harmed people of color by suggesting that unity within the Democratic party had to come at the expense of justice. I called it out on a group message chat when I was asked to do so by a number of women of color who were afraid to speak up for fear of being attacked. In the intervening days, as the conversation exploded, with some coming to the defense of the leader, and Black folx and allies continuing to speak to the harm, I was, to put it mildly, uncomfortable.

Why? Because challenging power, reconciling with power, is *always* uncomfortable.

Over time, I'd become used to the reactions in my body to this kind of discomfort. It's a profound desire to flee, to self-protect, to shut down. For me, it lives in my solar plexus, which tightens to the point of cutting off my breathing in all but the shallowest of forms. I've learned to recognize it, breathe through it, and sit with the discomfort in recognition of it, because capitulating to it is a capitulation to white supremacy. As with patriarchy, white supremacy wants us afraid, wants us scared, wants us silent, wants us complicit. Refusing to do that, and staying present instead so we can continue to reconcile with power and privilege, is critical work.

As I stayed in community with the women of color in the group, listening and not speaking for them unless I was asked to do so, I sat with my discomfort and refused to let this person off the hook. The disappointment and letdown among women of color in the group was palpable, and it hurt. My discomfort was a small price to pay for being a requested voice and ally that sought to call the leader in. I stayed true to myself and to those friends by continuing to speak through the discomfort—even and including when my words didn't initially change the outcome. Fortunately enough, within a few weeks, the leader did indeed recognize that there can be no unity without justice and accountability, and publicly shifted their perspective to reflect that, which was a step in right direction.

These lessons continue to work on me and push me to do more. If I can't be uncomfortable with being challenged to self-examine or with holding others accountable, I am a part of the problem instead of the solution. Similarly, if I run from discomfort instead of leveraging my privilege on behalf of those who have less of it, I am complicit in their oppression.

Hard conversations will not kill us, but refusing to have them may kill others or even us by enabling systemic and interpersonal oppression to thrive. We must learn to breathe through hard conversations, staying present in our discomfort and focused on the bigger goals of change and accountability, refrain from becoming defensive, and understand that we must walk in truth. Truth is often painful, but it is also, as the old saying goes, the path to freedom.

Reconciling with others and with ourselves requires honesty.

And honesty, real honesty and real accountability that leads to real change, is like rain: it washes away what hurts.

The song we sang to Megan as she lay dying, "Saint Honesty" by Sara Bareilles, says the following:

> We're collecting evidence of one remarkable storm
> How wild it was to find it, to finally feel the climate, instead
>   of only staying dry and warm.

If we do not bring the rain, if we do not bring the storm and be present to the swirling, terrifying winds of change, we stay dry instead in a safety that is not only a lie, a myth of a just society that doesn't exist, but that is also actually harmful and violent.

We must weather storms that change us. We can't settle for silence. We must speak, accept the challenges of creating a better world, and commit to truth that sets us free.

Let it rain.

11.

Amends

Seventeen years ago, I was asked to sit on a panel at UNC law school on the topic of reparations. At the time, I was working on a human rights case on behalf of women who had been kidnapped and forced to be sex slaves to the Japanese military during World War II. At the time, reparations were one form of justice we were discussing in our case, and I was privileged to sit on that panel with others who were advocating for reparations for slavery and across a wide swath of prior human rights abuses.

At the time, the concept of reparations for slavery or Indigenous genocide in America felt like a far-fetched hope. Public discussions of white supremacy and white privilege seemed to be next to nonexistent in any place but critical race theory classes in some universities. It wasn't until Ta-Nehisi Coates's seminal 2014 piece in *The Atlantic*, titled "The Case for Reparations," that I recall having any conversations about reparations anywhere outside of a law firm or law school debate.

In 2003, though, the barrage of questions from the audience for this panel were predictable.

"I was born poor and white, and I never had anything. Why should I be responsible for paying reparations for something I had nothing to do with?"

"Slavery is ancient history. People should just get over it."

"Isn't affirmative action enough?"

I hope by now you're at a place where you, along with most Americans, recognize how outrageous these statements sound, and that the effects of our original sins in this nation live on to this day. Those effects include wealth disparity, lack of advancement, unequal pay, education disparities, discrimination in access to health care, systemic racism in criminal justice and law—every aspect, truly, of our culture, that fails to treat Black, brown, and Indigenous people as equal. The work of reparation, reconciliation, and restorative justice is not just necessary, it's long overdue.

All of us have work to do, collaboratively and in coalition, to get us there. Whether you advocate for reparations by calling your congressperson, or get involved by bringing a racial justice curriculum to your local elementary school, in every industry and every corner of our society, there is work to be done. Each one of us can make a difference, and no work that pushes toward freedom is wasted. We all have to meet the call.

Heroines lift one another up, restore dignity and justice, work for the benefit of the collective and not just for themselves. Part of that is by making amends when needed, both at the most interpersonal level and by advocating for and cultivating amends in the world at large.

APOLOGIES COST NOTHING

You'll recall that, as I said earlier, perfectionism is a tool of oppression. None of us is perfect. All of us, and particularly those of us engaged in the work of unlearning what white supremacist patriarchy has taught us, will inevitably, at some point, fuck up. Maybe we fail to advocate when we should. Maybe, worse yet, we are ignorant and cause harm. Maybe we have internalized white supremacy and have turned it on ourselves and others. Maybe we haven't apologized for a serious wound we know we caused years ago that we'd like to repair.

Part of doing the work of amends is knowing when to apologize. Notably, this may not get you absolution. Particularly if what you're apologizing for is a harm that stems from your privilege, you must understand that whether you'll be forgiven is not up to you. It's up to the person you've harmed to evaluate whether or not your amends deserve that. But it doesn't change the fact that making amends is necessary, and you should do it as soon as you know you need to.

Particularly around harm that comes from privilege, many of us run from responsibility. It may not be as overt as the questions the panelists received in the example discussed earlier, but we may make excuses, or seek to minimize the harm we caused, or find ways of deflecting blame. This, too, is fragility. We can't grow, change, and model to others how it's done if we don't accept responsibility for the damage we cause.

Over the years, I've come to recognize that there is actually a lot of good work to be done in making amends. It always helps to offer an apology when we've caused pain, even unintentionally.

Reminder: impact matters more than intent, and when you've harmed someone, it doesn't matter if you didn't intend to. (I'm reminded of the boyfriend who cheated on me, and when I got upset said, "But I never intended to hurt you," which, of course, didn't change the fact that he did.) Offer amends whenever you know you need to do so. Note, though, that while the amends may not be accepted, running from responsibility and from our blind spots prolongs pain. It's much easier to simply and unequivocally apologize, take responsibility, and promise to do better. "I blew it, I'm sorry for the harm I caused, I take total responsibility, and I won't do it again" goes a long way.

While I've had to do this on a number of occasions publicly, I've also done it privately in close relationships. I can tell you that in a workplace or in intimate relationships, it's really important once you've offered amends to listen in response. You may be offered suggestions as to how to learn or proceed. You may be asked to witness the pain you've caused. Or, you may be told it wasn't as bad as you might have thought. Regardless, please offer the respect of listening, actively and attentively, to what is offered to you in return, and take it in. That includes when the response is "I can't accept your apology, and here's why." It will be uncomfortable, and as you know by now, part of the work is getting comfortable with discomfort.

As we've already discussed, as you reconcile with your own internalized bias, you *will* make mistakes. For this reason, getting practiced in apologizing and making amends instantly is a good idea. Giving yourself grace as you learn is also important. But remember, what we are striving for at this stage of reconciliation is doing all the work it takes to repair harm. Keep going. Don't quit. The discomfort you feel at your own failings is *nothing, I promise you*, compared with the harm that systemic and internalized oppression has done to anyone marginalized over centuries.

Owning your own shit helps others to do the same. Repairing the damage you've caused leads to healing. And from there, we can all move forward toward healing the world.

WORKING FOR AMENDS TO HISTORIC HARMS

In the next section, we're moving into the space of revolutionary change across institutions and systems of oppression. We can't leave amends, however, without discussing the profound need for restoration for, and reconciliation with, the gravest forms of institutional and systemic harm.

Collectively, we must realize that at the root of America is the genocide of Indigenous people. We who are not Indigenous are here because the land we live on was stolen. In the process, white colonizers nearly eradicated Indigenous tribes from this land, and the descendants of those who survived live with the impact of that to this day. As well, this entire nation was built on the labor of enslaved Africans, who were tortured, beaten, raped, and worked to death for the benefit of white American capitalism. This nation engaged in family separation of both Indigenous and enslaved persons for hundreds of years. The violence of the birth of this nation, the blood that seeped into the land on which we now stand, has never been remediated or redressed.

We have a unique opportunity at this moment in history to work to make amends—financial, equitable, spiritual, cultural— to reconcile these original harms. We must understand that in collective, refusing to look at these wounds, clean them, heal them, will allow them to fester forever. We need reparations for the descendants of enslaved persons. We need reparations for Indigenous tribes. We need to tell the truth about our history, not engage in mythologizing about manifest destiny and American exceptionalism. We must alter our view as a culture of what real amends look like, and live into it at every turn. Anything less is complicity.

If there is any aspect of purgatory that we can take from the tale of the Daughters of Danaus, the inability to wash oneself clean for all time feels rich in this instance. Absent the willingness to acknowledge the blood in this land and the harm at the root of our national origin, absent a real reckoning and real and ongoing healing and redress, we will be stuck forever in a cycle that can never make room for another way of being, where inequity and white supremacy will always reign. The ongoing harm will continue in unforgivable ways until we address it head on.

We must rise to the challenge this moment presents. We must reconcile with the unredressed cracks at our foundation of this nation, in our institutions, and in our own lives.

I urge you in this turning point of the journey to commit to making amends in every aspect of your life where you know you need to do so. Examine your own privilege, wherever it lies, and consider what taking action to redress it looks like. Commit to the truth in every path you walk. Commit to accountability and repair. Step forward bravely and do not run away. Do not take your eyes off the end goal: freedom, equity, justice for every one of us, for as long as it takes.

We've got work to do.

12.

Moving Toward Equity

Over the past decade, particularly with long-term clients with whom I've built relationships, I've been asked from time to time if I could teach all-encompassing diversity and inclusion workshops. Until the last few years, my answer was always yes, not only because I needed the work but also because I felt qualified to do the work. Now, though, I refer those requests to Black women colleagues instead.

Why? Just because I *can* accept that work doesn't mean that I *should*. Equity requires centering on marginalized voices, and one way to dismantle privilege is to uplift the voices of those who aren't traditionally heard.

One of the unfortunate things I've learned over the years about the corporate world is that diversity, equity, and inclusion ("DEI") work done therein is often used to placate vocal advocates within the organization, rather than to change the culture or actually create equity. Moreover, hard truths such as those I've told in certain workshops are often not actually welcome (more on that in the next section). Lastly, and most importantly, some organizations just prefer to hire white women to do this work, don't consider or aren't invested in supporting Black women in their consulting vendor base, or don't care to do the work of finding consultants who are diverse to do their DEI work.

These organizations have a problem, but aren't invested in actually fixing it in real, equitable ways, including by hiring diverse consultants and paying them equitably.

Here, we confront an example of how sometimes, living into equity means *not* doing. Just because I am offered that work doesn't mean I should take it. Rather, in order to live more fully into principles of equity, centering that work on the great Black women I know who are doing it is a means of leveraging my privilege for the change I wish to create in the world, and leveling the playing field.

Now, you may wonder why anyone would turn down paid work, and that in and of itself may feel like privilege. I certainly have had moments where my bank account was next to nothing and the next client opportunity couldn't come soon enough. But here's the thing: we who are accustomed to privilege, wherever we have it, have an obligation to leverage that privilege when we can to benefit those who do not share it, and to undermine it however we can. For me, part of moving toward equity means not just teaching others about equity, but actually allowing equity to govern who teaches about equity in the first place, and supporting institutions to make that decision even when it means I don't do the work. That means letting Black, brown, and Indigenous women lead on issues of racial equity and inclusion.

This brings me to a key point on moving toward equity for those of us who benefit from privilege: creating equity may *feel like loss* to those of us who have always experienced greater access, money, or benefits conferred by privilege as others gain access to power. As the saying goes, "For those who are accustomed to privilege, equality feels like loss."

When you're used to being able to talk your way into a job you're not qualified for, for instance, as many white men have done over centuries, saying instead, "I'm not qualified for this job, and think you should interview this person of color" can feel like giving up opportunity.

It's not. If benefits have been conferred on you unfairly because of systemic or structural oppression—and I'd argue that every white person in America has at some point benefited from the privileges conferred by white supremacy that are denied to others—giving up those benefits is actually a form of righting the apple cart.

A part of moving toward equity is consciously choosing to right that cart when you can. Ask yourself: Wherever you experience privilege, is there room for equity instead? How could you go about creating it? What could you do to cultivate it? Who might you need to listen to, instead of assuming you know the answer? How might you need to advocate? Do the nuanced investigation of what creating greater equity could look like, and proceed accordingly.

What feels like loss is actually a gain for all of us when we approach it from the perspective of value. Because real diversity and inclusion—to business, to leadership, and to the world, and the righting of structures that have cultivated privilege to the detriment of some of us—benefits all of us.

HOLDING THE DOOR

A few years ago, I was on a women's retreat where the conversation turned to ancient societies where women ruled—stories that in many instances have been relegated to the benches of history, hidden away in arcane volumes in dusty libraries, out of public view. One woman, an amateur student of matriarchal societies throughout history, began discussing the role of male guards in temples where women leaders ruled in collective.

In her examples, men played a particular but critical role in assuring that women were allowed to do the work of leading: those men were responsible for guarding the doors of the temple.

Notably, their guardianship took two forms: first, allowing access through the temple doors to the women who were there to lead, and second, guarding those temple doors to make sure that no one who posed a threat to those women could gain entry.

I've thought about this discussion hundreds of times since. While we'll spend some time in the next section of the book talking about revolution of oppressive systems, I'd like you to consider for a moment the role of the heroine in moving toward equity in daily life right now as one of holding the door.

Holding the door is a means of leveraging and dismantling privilege. Are you opening doors for historically marginalized people in places where you experience privilege? If you are white, do you work to promote women of color in your workplace? Do you recommend and foster great Black talent when you see it? If you are straight, do you work to create opportunities for greater representation of LGBTQ+ people in the halls of power? If you are able-bodied, do you think about how to create actual physical access for those who are not? Do you center on the voices of leaders who don't bear your privilege to show others how it's done? If so, you are doing your part in one aspect of holding the door.

On the flip side, are you a protector of those who don't bear your privileges? Do you use your voice to call out white supremacy where you see it in action? Do you uplift and protect leaders from marginalized communities that are not your own, and make sure that they are safe to do their critical work in the world? Inside your organization or political work, do you put your voice or your body on the line to keep all people safe? Do you work to contradict sabotage by others where you witness it? Are you a guardian of equity? This is another part of holding the door.

Those of us with privileges must hold the door relentlessly to those who don't share them if we are committed to making real change.

DOING THE WORK EVERYWHERE

In the next section, we're going to go deeper into how to undermine systemic oppression in your own life, at work, and in the world. For now, though, I'd like you to take an inventory of where you see inequity in your daily life. This can range from your most intimate spaces to the biggest public aspects. Start small and build outward.

Do you find yourself doing more of the housework, child care, and other traditionally feminine allocated tasks in your home? Do you find yourself relegated to administrative instead of power-player roles at work? Do you experience discrimination in pay, opportunity, education? Are you silenced in the civic organizations in which you operate in favor of white, male, or straight voices? Are you routinely afraid of systemic violence from the police, your government, or your fellow citizens?

Once you start looking at inequity and inequality as they play out in your own life, you can begin to see where the real work of revolution needs to take place. Identifying where the work needs to be done is just the tip of the iceberg.

Keep going. These are the seeds we are planting in the cremation ground. We are fertilizing them with our old trauma, ignorance, harms, and failures. We're reconciling with the work to be done.

We are bringing sunlight to the darkness that power depends upon to survive. And we have to bring the sunlight before we can bring the rain.

Section Three
Revolution

13.

The Letter and the Path

Imagine that one day, a letter arrives in your mailbox. "Dear Beloved One," it begins.

The letter starts by telling you a story about yourself—how you were born, how much you matter, how you became a part of the world. It tells you of the family you belong to, the wounds that existed for generations, the twisting path of DNA and choice and trauma and fate that led you here, of the legacy that made you.

And then it tells you this: for the rest of your days, without exception, you will be cared for unconditionally.

Should you need it, a baseline amount of money will be made available to you that guarantees your survival. You will always have a place to live. You will always have food to eat. You need not fear that you will end up dying alone on the street in your old age. You will be provided with the highest quality medical care available. You will not have to pay for it. Any education that you want, or that your children might want, will also be paid for. Best of all, everyone you know will also be given this—no matter where they were born or to whom, no matter the color of their skin or their gender or their national origin or how they came to live in the country you share. Moreover, if you are descended from enslaved persons or are Indigenous, you receive immediate, substantial reparations for the genocidal harms caused to your people. All at once, everyone, equally, can release the fear of not having enough. All at once, everyone, equally, can release the fear of not being enough. Everyone, equally and instantly, has value in the eyes of this society. Everyone matters.

Imagine what it would do for you to receive such a letter. Imagine what it would do for our entire society and culture for *everyone* to receive such a letter.

It would be, in a word, revolutionary.

And while it wouldn't rectify all culturally indoctrinated inequity in an instant—because white supremacist patriarchy exists in every aspect of our culture, after all—some things would change right away. An end to division, fear for one's own security and the security of one's children. An end to poverty. An end to vulnerability to fascism, hate, rage that can be exploited by evil personalities to divide and destroy. An end to the terror of the pie being too small for everyone but the lauded few, rather than enough, always, for everyone.

It would mean the dismantling of American exceptionalism and rugged individualism, in favor of something greater. It would mean a collective human identity that accounts for diversity and the value of all human beings.

If it wouldn't change much for you, you are profoundly privileged and have an even greater obligation to work for equity.

Because for many of us, it would change everything, for good.

◊◊

The word *revolution* has its origins in the Latin word *revolvere*, meaning "to revolve." According to *Merriam-Webster*, when *revolution* first appeared in English in the fourteenth century, it referred to "the movement of a celestial body in orbit"; that sense was extended to "a progressive motion of a body around an axis," "completion of a course." The word also developed a different meaning, namely, "a sudden radical, or complete change," apparently from the idea of reversal of direction implicit in the Latin verb. *Revolt*, which initially meant "to renounce allegiance," grew from the same idea of "rolling back," in this case from a prior bond of loyalty.

Revolution, in other words, is the rolling forward of beliefs, society, cultures. It is the renunciation of allegiance to systems or institutions that we once tolerated. It is the completion of cycles that no longer serve us. It is stepping onto another, new cycle of the journey—yours as a heroine or ours as a collective—to renounce what isn't working, and to revolve toward something new. It is the spiral of successive generations, manifest in the cover of this book, once again committing to making the world a better place, over and over again, and refusing to stand down in the face of injustice.

Notably, revolution doesn't require the armed overthrow of government or institutions. As the BBC reported in 2019, violence doesn't usually work to create long-term change. Nonviolent protests are in fact twice as likely to succeed as armed conflict, and it takes a threshold of just 3.5 percent of the population to bring about real and serious change.

I personally don't have trouble imagining that the 3.5 percent that it takes is us.

Revolution is the tilling, the aerating of the soil in the cremation ground. It's the turning of the seasons, the changing of the wind, that brings new life to the vision of what is possible. It lives on the sudden change in the weather, the rustling of leaves on the patio, in the sweeping in of the clouds from the ocean to right over this house where I now sit, just before the rain. It is the willingness to turn, and turn again, and turn again, for as long as it takes, toward that which is better, more just, more destined to lead to the path to freedom.

Revolution is within you and outside of you, connected in all things. It is yours and it is all of ours. We cycle through it again and again. We walk the path of the heroine's journey over and over, each orbit bringing change within and without. We live in this space, turning over the ground, tilling it for growth, until the perfect conditions exist for rebirth. We call the clouds and the weather to ripen the conditions. We walk the path as we carve new grooves in our thinking and in our actions, renouncing those that are no longer useful or never were, to bring about revolutionary change.

Imagine all that we could heal, in an instant, simply by deciding collectively that it was time to revolve toward a new way of being, a new culture of equity, care, and, dare I say it, love. Imagine what it would be like to open that letter.

Imagine, further still, what it would be like to be the one who gets to send it.

Imagine how lucky you would be to be the wind, the harbinger, that calls on that change.

14.

Putting It All
on the Line

n the months leading up to the 2016 election, I was writing a
lot—pages upon pages that I was posting on Facebook about the
law and ethics and politics and feminism and equity. I became so
prolific online, so determined to share what I knew and to sound
alarm bells of a pending Trump victory, that my old role as an
adjunct professor at Columbia Law School felt like it had become
more of a public mantle. While I was originally just talking to my
friends, strangers began to follow me online in larger and larger
numbers as I kept writing. Questions were posted on my feed routinely asking for guidance and insight and understanding. I did my
best to answer them as often as possible.

And then, of course, we lost.

Shortly after that, my friend Amanda Steinberg sent me a message that said, "Hey, have you heard of this new feature called
Facebook Live? You could just hit the button and start talking to

all of us about these issues, organizing us, motivating us into action, and save yourself all that writing." Hmm, I thought. Maybe.

I tested out this new feature a few times—first live-streaming a protest outside the Brooklyn federal courthouse on the night the travel ban was stayed, and then a few more times, taking live questions from friends and viewers.

Over the earliest weeks of 2017, this quickly became a daily occurrence. Initially, this live broadcast had no name—it was just a way for me to easily talk to my friends and a few others about what was happening in the early days of the Trump administration, to educate and empower and organize. At the time, my Facebook feed numbered around 2,500 people. The broadcast was off-the-cuff, very raw, and created from my dining room table on my iPhone every day at 11 a.m.

What happened next was not something I anticipated, planned, or asked for. Someone, still unknown to me, dropped one of my broadcasts into the main Pantsuit Nation group on Facebook, which had more than 3.5 million Hillary Clinton supporters at that point. Within a matter of days, my broadcast went viral. Within a few months, it was clocking up to a hundred thousand viewers a day.

Thus, #ResistanceLive was born.

By that time, however, I'd spent the better part of six years building a consulting company on women's leadership, and emotionally intelligent leadership generally, from the ground up. Our clients included some of the most conservative investment banks in the country, law firms, private equity firms, hedge funds. And yet here I was, suddenly and very unexpectedly, railing on the daily against the Trump administration and its policies, advocating for impeachment, and, it should be said, *swearing a lot*. This came as no surprise to my friends, but to my COO? Who'd signed on to work for a company dedicated to advancing women's leadership in corporate environments and who was tracking our client invoices and contracts? Not so much.

Sure enough, a few months into #ResistanceLive going viral, I got a call from that COO. She cut straight to the chase.

"You have to stop doing this," she said. "Hundreds of thousands of dollars of contracts are on the line." I was being recognized in airports, at the supermarket, even on the streets of New York City just taking a walk with my kids, she pointed out. "What will we do when one of our clients discovers the broadcast, and objects, or worse yet, pulls their business?"

"We could lose everything," she said.

I took a deep breath, and paused, and then gave the only answer that I could.

"I don't care. We're going to keep going anyway."

I tried to explain why. The broadcast had a pull, an energetic hook into my solar plexus—*it felt like a calling*. It didn't feel like work, ever, and still doesn't. It didn't feel like an obligation. Rather, it felt like an invitation to something far bigger than myself, an offer that could not be refused, *an act of service that called me on*. It just simply, and with utter clarity, could not be denied.

That moment was the closest I had ever come to feeling like I had discovered my reason for being, at least to that point. And the broadcast was without question one of the most critical efforts, one of the most critical means, for returning my gifts to collective use.

There was never any question in my mind, not once, that if the broadcast cost me clients, or cost me money, or even forced me to go back to the daily practice of law, it would be worth it. And that has proven to be right. In the almost five years since, thousands of listeners have told me that #ResistanceLive has taught them that they could make a difference, that their voice mattered, that they could create change, become activists when they had never done so before, organize protests and phone banking and postcard drives, get out the vote, run for office, learn how to step into something bigger, live into a real mission, and motivate others to do the same. It changed lives. It built a movement (more than one, actually). It turned ordinary people into warriors for justice and into heroines in their own lives, communities, and the world.

The audience that found me, quite organically, needed this, and I needed them. The strange path of my career—from my work as an activist, to my experience as an advocate and litigator and a law professor at Columbia, to my ability to communicate knowledge in layperson's language that non-lawyers could understand, to my skills as an executive coach and thought leader that led others to clear the debris of internalized silencing so that their gifts could be offered back in the form of action—all this which had always felt so disjointed and out of the ordinary suddenly made perfect sense. Everything I'd ever done had led to this point.

Moreover, something inexplicable was sometimes happening on the broadcast. The only way to describe it was that it felt like becoming something else, something otherworldly at times, as though I were a catalyst and a conduit through which something larger flowed. It was very much *not about me*. Sometimes, I would log on to the broadcast with just a list of topics, and without thinking much, the words would just pour out of me. The experience of turning off any internal limits that would have prevented me from doing this, and just allowing my gifts to be used in this way, felt like the highest form of my purpose and being. It was an opportunity for which I was profoundly grateful. It healed something in me, a long-standing view of my inadequacies and perceived failure at having left a more traditional path, and it all suddenly integrated into something bigger and gave me all the whys I'd ever needed. With the most epic, undeniable clarity, *it would not be denied.*

My COO did not like this. And in a sense, I can't blame her. She wasn't ready for the ride of us, the suddenly enormous public profile, the entirely bizarre experience of my internet celebrity, the controversy, the targets it put on our doorstep, the stalkers, and the sometimes *very* overt efforts to destroy the company that came with it. She wasn't ready for the fluctuations it brought to our business model on top of it. She preferred the more vanilla aspects of working inside the master's house, as opposed to the revolutionary pull toward change.

And though her work was excellent, and though she stuck around for a few more months, it wasn't long before we decided to go our separate ways. And that's OK. I kept going.

In the years since, ironically enough, what she feared the most has actually come to pass, and on more than one occasion. I have indeed had corporate clients—mostly women, in particular—who found #ResistanceLive. Curiously enough, it furthered their interest in our work, rather than stymied it, and led to even greater clarity in terms of what we had to offer them. The broadcast created a new level of resonance with what we as a company could provide to women who were seeking the means and the skills to become change agents in their own environments, to create revolutions right where they lived.

And while our business model certainly shifted again during the pandemic, and evolved as I evolved, I found that, in the long run, the cost of putting myself out there, while real, was not overwhelming in most cases. It was counterbalanced, moreover, by the tremendous joy of living in complete integrity with my values, in alignment with my purpose, and for the greater good. I get to live daily in a space of hope and honesty and integrity and growth— not always easy but always rewarding—and in a community of like-minded activists and friends that benefit daily from what I have to offer. In return, and even at key points of crisis, it has offered me more support than I could have previously imagined and a lot of love that I never expected to come my way.

I put it all on the line to be a part of the work of revolution at a critical time in history, for myself, for our community, and for the future. I'd do it all again in a heartbeat.

RUNNING ON FAITH

That is not to say that it was always easy, or that I was 100 percent certain that it made sense. Most of the time, I was running on faith.

What do I mean by that? I mean that for a long time, I didn't have any clue as to what the broadcast might lead to, nor whether it would be a help or a hindrance, nor what it would mean for me professionally. I had no idea if it would ever benefit me under traditional metrics of success, like money or greater opportunities for professional growth. For the first two years of the broadcast, we did it completely for free, despite the epic amount of work and cost we had to offset from the company to do it. I kept going anyway. In my gut, I knew that there had to be an end game, but I couldn't see it. I was running on faith.

The state of running on faith may be a familiar one to you. It's a partner to the moment that can't be refused despite advice to the contrary, to the offer you know you must accept though you don't know why, to the invitation you know you must decline because better things await though you might not know what they are. It's the place that calls you into the unknown, when you can't envision the path. It is *trust*, of the highest order, that there is a reason for the fork in the road, even when you can't see where the path might lead.

Now, it helps if you believe, as I do, that there are no wrong choices on the heroine's journey. You are exactly where you are supposed to be at this moment. There is no "late" and there is no "behind." Every challenge you might face has something to teach you. Every victory pushes you forward on the path to growth.

Everything you are has brought you to this place of revolution, to this place on the path where things will turn, and where you will be an agent of the turning.

Knowing when and how to become that change agent, when and how to put it all on the line, is a matter of profound inner knowing. Revolution, and the choice to engage with it and to take risks to create change, requires the cultivation of your faith in yourself, and in your capacity to make choices that move you forward.

In the best advice I've ever received, my father once characterized this turning point to me as a "sacred obligation to make choices that move you forward." I would add, for purposes of this discussion, that it is *also* your sacred obligation to make choices that benefit the whole of us, rather than just ourselves or a lauded few.

This is how revolution begins: you claim the sacred obligation to yourself and to your community to make choices that move us forward, at the exact moment when you know you should.

INTUITION

Cultivating your inner knowing is a skill. Trusting our inner knowing is something that structures of oppression want to train or beat out of us, because our intuition is a threat. Indeed, the collective knowledge of women generally, and our storytelling and inner knowing, heal others and heal the planet. It's so dangerous to those in power that at certain times in history, it's gotten us burned at the stake.

Your intuition may be the most critical faculty you have in deciding when to put it all on the line. If you work it, you will know where your voice is most needed; how and when to use it; and when you need to leave, run, or fight. If you trust that your intuition will never do you wrong, you will have the most effective weapon you need to create change, wherever you choose to apply it. Though it may seem esoteric, it's the long work of heroines to use skills that are historically ignored or dismissed to achieve seemingly insurmountable ends. Underestimate us at your peril, in other words.

My work spans not just leadership, but also the realms of myth and archetypes and spiritual practice for exactly this reason. Revolutionary work requires every skill imaginable, and the confidence to apply the right skill at the right moment. Thus, I encourage you to do the work of training your intuition into a finely tuned instrument.

If this work is new to you, feel free to start small. Leave your house on a walk with no destination in mind. At every crossroads, pause, and listen to where your inner knowing wants to take you. Along the way, pay attention to signs, objects, messages that enter your field of vision. Use this as a meditative practice. You will find that you never end up in the wrong place.

Over time, you can continue this practice by setting out on a walk or into a meditation with a question for which you need an answer. I did this once in New York City, only to turn a corner after a long meditative walk to find myself in front of the New Museum, where a two-story HELL YEAH! had been installed on the front of the building. The answer to the question I'd started with was therefore obvious, and you should demand *very obvious signs* if you enter this practice thinking you might miss something. Trust me, this works, though for some it takes more practice than for others.

The journey of modern heroines requires remembering that for centuries we were in touch with the elements, the stars, with nature as our guides. We've lost those skills over time, but they are latent in our DNA. Turn on the right switch, and you'll find that when it comes to putting it all on the line, you are more ready than you might have suspected, and more armed for the battle than our oppressors want to admit.

Trust yourself. You have everything you need, right now, and you have from the beginning. You are here for a big purpose and as a part of a collective mission. You will know the moment that calls you when you know yourself.

RISK AND SACRIFICE

Change requires risk. As we've discussed already, if we aren't willing to risk something, anything, for change, we are in fact engaged in preserving the status quo. Revolution, moreover, is uncomfortable. When we think of armed revolutions, lives are put on the line for change, and not everyone makes it. Our revolution may be a nonviolent one, but that doesn't mean it's going to be easy. At this pivotal moment in history, our discomfort and fear in the face of old systems of oppression are a sign that we are on the right path.

Particularly with regard to undermining privilege, I must remind you that revolution, and putting it all on the line for change, may feel like loss. You may have to give up the idea that you haven't internalized white supremacy, or that your privileges came just from hard work or smarts and not also because you have the benefit of being white, heterosexual, cis, and/or able-bodied, or that your achievements aren't inherently and historically dependent on the labor of others. You may have to abandon your perception that you are exceptional, or that the access or the power that you've been granted isn't conditional on your willingness to be complicit in maintaining the status quo wherever your privilege lies. And you will most likely have to abandon some form of the power that's been irrationally granted to you in exchange for the willingness to remain silent while others are oppressed. Revolutionary change will require your discomfort, because we can't change structures of oppression without abandoning the selective benefits they provide to some, but not all.

But I'd remind you here to have some perspective. If you are a white woman, for instance, your feelings are nothing compared with centuries of systemic oppression, slavery, and genocide, and further, to be blunt about it, centering on your feelings in the face of discussions of race and justice is actually a form of internalized bias. Centering on our feelings—or for that matter on our activist history, or on how busy or overwhelmed we are when we're called to allyship, accountability, or the need for revolutionary change— is structural oppression working through us to shut the conversation down. Wherever you have benefited personally in exchange for systemic oppression working on others, your obligation is to revolve those systems, and it is *work*.

In light of that, I'd encourage you to spend some time privately or in conversation with others bearing your privileges, and consider how you're going to avoid centering on your own discomfort rather than those harmed, so that you do not cause further harm on the path to wanting to create change. What are you willing to give up in order to create justice and change for those to whom it has been denied? How will you hold the door even when it's uncomfortable? How are you going to advocate and work for justice even if and when it costs you comfort?

Revolutionary change toward the freedom and equity of all requires us to actually get equal. It's hard work, but we are here to do hard things. Let's go.

BUT WHAT IF I FAIL?

Right around the time that I was finishing up this book, I got a call from a major corporate client. I'd worked with this company, a

Wall Street bank, for the better part of four years at that point, including several consecutive years of diversity and inclusion seminars. As usual, when the time came for annual scheduling, I reached out to confirm that we were still on for our diversity and inclusion training for new hires that year.

For as long as I'd worked with this client, diversity and inclusion had been a real problem. Only 14 percent of their senior leadership were women. Only one of their worldwide managing directors was a person of color. None of the senior leadership identified publicly as LGBTQ+. And despite a worldwide presence, there was seemingly little recognition of the eventual financial impact the bank was likely to experience in the coming years by failing to rectify its lack of inclusion, as more and more of its clients demanded diversity profiles in their service providers, investors, and buy/sell teams.

A few days after my annual inquiry about scheduling, I got a phone call from one of the senior leaders I'd worked with over the years. Though it had been nine months since the last diversity training I'd run, she had some feedback to provide me, and sad news to deliver: despite all the time and money they'd already invested and despite our long-standing professional relationships, the firm would not be bringing me back again.

What happened next was a real lesson in the entrenched nature of racism and sexism in institutions.

To back up for a minute: I didn't remember much about the prior year's seminar beyond the fact that there had been some pushback in the room from a few young white men. Particularly, I remembered a group of them in a corner of the room, a little snarly and inappropriately laughing, who from the start didn't seem to think something like a diversity and inclusion session was particularly warranted. I am used to young men like these—and came armed with my battery of de-escalating tools—humor, acknowledgment, attention, accountability, and smarts. Notably, in this room of about 110 folks, there were only a handful of Asian Americans, a handful of women, and one Black man. The remainder were young white men just out of college and destined for a career in finance. And it should be said that the content I covered was identical to what had been covered in past years, down to the identical PowerPoint deck, which had been routinely met with positive reviews.

This particular crew of young white men in the corner that day were a bit notable for their note-passing and laughing as I taught, as well as for the way in which they took up space. There was a lot of sprawling across trainee chairs, and spread legs and gum-chewing as I went through the material—much of which paralleled the opening of this book on issues of systemic, institutional, interpersonal, and internalized bias. During the training, as I always do, and in the context of systemic racism, I covered why reverse racism is a fabrication—in that racism is systemic and institutional, and about power, and if you understand that, you understand why there is no such thing as reverse racism in our culture, or reverse sexism for that matter.

I fielded some curious questions in that training from the boys in the corner. One challenged the idea that the imposter complex was based in patriarchy, because occasionally he himself had felt inadequate. I responded by discussing how there's a difference between a basic learning curve that we all might face and systems of inequality that are designed to undermine your success by messaging you from early childhood that you are less-than. Another young man explicitly challenged the idea that white people had internalized racism, period, despite a long discussion about how we're all the products of our culture.

At the end of the training, however, I was approached by the one Black man who had been in the room who needed my help, and his white male friend who was an ally, and I was able to intervene on his behalf to resolve an issue (more on that below). That left me feeling that, on the whole, the training had opened minds and doors. Fundamentally, moreover, I'd faced far more hostile environments in other trainings, and this one didn't feel particularly unusual.

The following day, I had run a women's leadership program for just the young women trainees who had been in the room. Several noted that there was an obvious "bro culture" at play in the men in the trainee class, and that already they'd heard some shockingly sexist comments that had frightened them about what was to come. Pointed reference was made to the group in the corner of the room the day prior, and how they'd intimidated others. I strategized with a few of the female hires after that day's seminar on how to address those comments interpersonally and within the institution, and reported back to my internal colleagues on outcomes—again not anything unusual—and then caught my flight home feeling good about our programming, with no negative feedback.

Fast forward to this conversation nine months later concerning program renewal. The senior leader with whom I'd worked for so long began to share the feedback she'd received. As she spoke, a shocking set of facts began to present themselves.

Of the 110 or so trainees in the room, only about a third had filled out a review. Of those who did, however, there was an obvious consistency in the commentary, too coordinated to ignore. The comments ranged from "it's a bold statement that all white people are racist," to "reverse racism is real," to "she dismissed my question about the imposter complex, which men have, too" to "this was a shoddy take on important topics that made it sound like all white men are racist," to "dismissive in the extreme to men who asked questions." Rankings of my program, in direct opposition to prior years, ranged from "poor" to "adequate" for the majority of surveys. The bros, in other words, had executed a coordinated takedown.

As the feedback was read to me over the phone, I sighed. I responded to my internal colleague that the material was the same as in years past, that I dealt with young white men who were uncomfortable with the material in other environments, and that occasionally this sort of thing occurred and it was up to the institution to decide whether to endorse and entertain it.

Unfortunately, and despite years of quality work, these young white men had used their voices to object to diversity and inclusion and were validated by leadership's response, and I would not be returning to the company to train again, despite our long and positive relationship over the past years.

᠎᠎

So here's the thing about this story: it's not at all out of the ordinary. Particularly in traditionally masculine professions, those who challenge the status quo often pay a price. Bias is entrenched, certain voices are uplifted while others are silenced, and those of power and privilege are loath to accept that something other than what the exceptionalism they've been told they embody is the cause of their success. Indeed, in a recent interview I conducted with Marianne Cooper, a sociologist at the Stanford VMware Women's Leadership Innovation Lab, said that for gender-based initiatives to succeed, it is critical that *leaders* and institutions address privilege. Such conversations are challenging, she explained, because when people are confronted about their privilege, they often react defensively, which can then undermine their support for diversity efforts, even in the face of the evidence of the bottom-line cost.

To that end, this is a good time to tell you that, in any effort to realign power and create revolutionary change, you *will* fail at some point, perhaps even spectacularly, and you will pay a price. That price may be small or it may be large—indeed, my past business with the client referenced above had generated hundreds of thousands of dollars in revenue for my company over a period of many years. Others I know have had the usual "too pushy," "too loud" feedback dropped into a performance review when they've gone to bat for change in their place of work. None of this should come as a surprise, because power doesn't like to share, and most of those in power will fight to maintain it without even realizing their unconscious bias—which, cyclically, is all the more reason why we must keep opening hearts and minds, and fighting back.

That said, there are two questions to ask yourself when an effort to effect change fails:

1. Was the effort worth it?
2. What am I going to do next?

When I turn these questions on the circumstance where my long-standing corporate client did not renew our diversity training, I don't find myself thinking of that crew of young white men rooted in their privilege so much as the young Black man who approached me with his white ally after the seminar was over. You see, the help he needed from me was actually the result of a devastating discovery—he'd found out the night before that the company was paying him five thousand dollars a year less than all the white hires in the room and, shockingly, that he'd been put through a qualifying exam that no white candidate had been asked to take. Through my connections to senior leadership at the company, I was able to immediately go to bat for him and to document the discrimination that had occurred in his hiring and pay process in the event. By the following day, he'd been given a raise that brought him to equal pay, and I'd had a conversation with senior leadership about the discriminatory process that had led to his exam, with a promise that an investigation would ensue.

Now, I don't tell this story for "cookies," as they say, nor through the lens of white saviorism. In fact, I didn't tell this story *to anyone* until the day that I was fired from the gig nine months later. However, in the reflection to myself of losing the gig for what I said on the dais versus assisting this young man in obtaining equal pay and an investigation of his treatment, the answer to the question "Was it worth it?" is unquestionably yes. For that young man, and for others in the room who didn't fill out the survey, the answer is yes. For the women in the next day's seminar concerned about bro culture, to whom I could provide some guidance, the answer is yes. For the unknown ripple effects of my work inside the institution, even in light of the outcome for me personally, the answer is yes. And there's not a whit of doubt in my mind that I'd do it the same way all over again.

"What do I do next?" was a harder question. The loss of the

client came at a time when our business model was shifting, and I was wondering whether we'd ever be making money in corporate again given my outspoken political and advocacy work, and how that reflected in the highest levels of the corporate world. And a few months later, we were in the middle of a pandemic that would have changed it all anyway.

What I did, in the end, was sit down to write this book. And as I told the story here, and processed it through this lens, the answer became clear: what to do next was reach a wider audience, with the same message, to effect even greater change.

We keep going. When faced with a setback or a failure to effect a version of change we'd hoped for, we find new routes, new means to create change, and we keep going.

At certain moments these days I find myself thinking a lot about civil rights leaders of generations past, and civil rights leaders of the present, and the ongoing struggle to effect change that those fighting for it did not live to witness. We may not see the change we wish to see next week or next year or even in our lifetimes. That doesn't make the struggle for change any less worthy, or the revolution we cultivate any less important. And though the cost of battle may at times be quite high, we have one another, we have the call of justice, and we have the truth. As my friend La-Tosha Brown sings regularly and in the words of the great Ella Baker, "We who believe in freedom cannot rest until it comes."

Keep going. Even in the face of failure, keep going. Find the new way around, the new path, the new tools, because you are—and if you keep going, you will still be—a catalyst for change.

15.

Engaging Revolution: Policy and Politics

We've done a lot of work so far in this book to set the stage for this moment. Now, the time has come for all that we've incubated to emerge to push us forward to create revolutionary change—for us to step out where it matters most and lead.

In my view, the decision to do this isn't optional. All of us, every one, have places where we could be using our voices for change that benefits others, and perhaps ourselves, in the process. You're reading this book for a reason. Your calling is waiting for you. And at some point, an issue or a circumstance will demand (or has demanded) your action, and will not be denied. At some point, you will arrive at the place where, in the words of author Minda Harts, "Somebody's freedom is tied to you activating your voice."*

*Minda Harts (@MindaHarts), "Somebody's freedom is tied to you activating your voice . . . ," December 7, 2020, https://twitter.com/MindaHarts/status/1336053710108155914?s=20.

Chances are good that if you've read the entire book up until now, rather than just opened up to this section, you already know what you need to do. But if not, now's the time to decide where you want to see and create revolutionary change. Consider your trajectory right now—personally, professionally, or in the world. Where do you know you could be elevating your voice or the voices of others to effect change? Where have you not done enough? Where will you choose, right now, to dedicate your time and your actions to create revolutionary change? How will you be the catalyst?

For the thousands of women I've coached over the past decade, this process is both personal and political. For some, this has meant running for office. For others, it has meant nationwide, hardcore organizing in the streets for Black lives. For still more, it has meant going to detention camps at the border to advocate, bear witness, and leverage truth for justice in immigration policy. These have been massive, historic efforts on the part of these women to put their bodies, and sometimes their lives, on the line for real change.

Not all of us may be ready for something that big as a starting point, and that's OK. All of us are necessary to the cause of building an equitable and just society, so don't worry if your efforts in that direction may seem small at first. Perhaps the place that you decide to advocate for change is in your workplace. Maybe you choose to gust the winds of change toward unionizing at your job, or toward a new family leave policy that benefits workers, or toward gender and racial parity on a nonprofit board where you volunteer. Perhaps you dedicate time to the local school board advocating to protect marginalized kids from bullying. Maybe you participate in organizing programs at your school on gender equity, LGBTQ+ equity, or the rights of trans kids. Maybe you leverage your boss for an in-house equal pay analysis and equitable compensation at all tiers. Maybe you work with a local disability rights organization to bring greater accessibility to those in your community who need it. The options are endless.

And you need not choose every issue that speaks to you. I've long been an advocate for the theory that we must choose two to three issues that really matter to us, about which we are most lit up or the most devastated, to dedicate our energies. Others will choose the remainder. Trust that in collective, we will all bring oxygen and we will all bring the rain to every cause that needs it. Remember that we are each here with a unique set of gifts that will have an impact in unique ways. Choosing how and when and where to apply those gifts requires nuance. And of particular value in that arena is the issue of resonance: Where are your gifts most needed, and where will the impact of their deployment have the greatest and most rewarding effect?

The key here is to engage your passion and your talents in the push toward change on the issues that matter most to you, and where you know you can have the most impact, and then to not let go. For example, my entire life in some form or another has been a path for gender equality and racial justice. From that first anti-apartheid protest I organized at Harvard, to my work as a human rights lawyer, to the company I now run, every part of my life has spiraled back, over and over again, to fighting for equity and justice. Though the immediate focus may change, I know that injustice is a trigger for me, relentlessly, to continue to fight. Critically, I have been unable to be silent on these issues even when I knew the cost could be high. You should find the issues that feel that way to you.

That doesn't mean that you'll be able to make a massive impact on the first try, and it doesn't mean you won't need breaks from time to time. Indeed, stamina, consistency, and focus are critical arrows to the change agent's quiver. The terror field will appear to you over and over again. Sometimes you will fail. Sometimes you will succeed. But the key here is to never give up, because the only way that injustice will continue to reign is if we quit.

Remember, too, our earlier conversation about breakthrough movements. Be sure to build alliances with those who don't look or love like you do, particularly around common causes. Understand that real, groundbreaking, world-building change is going to require every one of us to do our part carrying that life-giving water. Be conscious that we have much to learn from one another, and be open to those who call out your blind spots. Turn pain into action, fear into work, and challenge into motivation. Keep going. We're all going to get there, together.

FLEXING THE COURAGE MUSCLE

Since the 2016 election, I've worked with women who never in a million years would have considered themselves to be activists before that moment. Having confronted their own lit Match, however, they were determined to create revolutionary change, even if it scared them and even if they'd never engaged in any work as change agents previously. Many of them started small—with a phone call to their representative to ask for an investigation, or a postcard writing campaign for the 2018 election, or by canvassing their neighbors for a candidate. Gradually, their comfort grew. Now, some of those women have organized citywide protests, managed entire campaigns, or even run for office themselves. The transformation has been an absolute blessing to witness in every case.

As these women did, at every step along the path to revolution, you will encounter your own terror field. Sometimes, your anger or outrage may overwhelm the fear, but it will be there, lurking underneath. For this reason, start the path of your own work in this regard outside your comfort zone as far as feels tolerable, but no more. I often analogize this to working for a deep stretch but not a hamstring tear. You want to push the boundaries of the possible, because no growth comes without it, but not so far that you lose your ability to strategize.

Every single person I've ever met who has strived for revolutionary change has been scared along the way. Yes, living on faith helps. Yes, knowing that you are on a path with purpose helps. It doesn't mean you're not scared at least some of the time. Again, we return to the lesson that we must feel the fear, and do it anyway. As with vulnerability and voice, every time it will get easier. Perhaps today you're fighting for greater diversity at your firm. Perhaps next month, you're on a stage telling your entire industry why representation matters so much. Perhaps next year, you're breaking out and starting your own firm, where equity and inclusion are built in from the ground up. Every step of the way, we revolve more toward justice, and away from what doesn't serve the whole.

Now, a key lesson for those of us with privilege: flexing the courage muscle doesn't always mean getting loud. Remember the lessons about holding the door: sometimes, your job is to listen, and let others (particularly Black, brown, and Indigenous women) lead.

Sometimes, courage lies in elevating others. Sometimes, courage is not centering on ourselves. Sometimes, courage is in taking the backseat when we've always charged in, thinking we knew best how to save the day.

And for all of us who are historically marginalized, the practice of using our voice for change is a progressive one. Each time, that courage muscle grows stronger. Each time, our voice becomes more confident. Each time, we look at people and whole systems designed to keep us down, and say, "Not today, Satan." Every time we do it, we claim power from those who would seek to deny us our right to walk free.

Again, like the path of the heroine, this process is lifelong. See the long game. Understand truly that, in the words of the famous MLK quote, "The arc of the moral universe is long, but it bends toward justice." You are a part of the force that is here to bend it, and your ability to do that grows exponentially the more courageous you become.

If you have truly done the work of uncovering your own biases, and working for revolutionary change that benefits all of us, you, too, will see yourself as a conduit, and the call will become undeniable. Champion change wherever it is required. Use your voice, your gifts, your energy, and your time on the issues that call to you the most. Understand that once you're on the path, you don't ever step off it, and every cycle, every revolution, brings another chance for change.

Keep going. Someone else's freedom, and indeed whole systems designed to prevent it, depend on you activating your voice.

A WORD ON REVOLUTIONARY REST

In the early fall of 2019, I found myself at a breaking point. That summer, in the space of a month, I'd worked in collaboration with a massive international group of activists, advocates, and leaders on immigration issues to organize a mobilization against the incarceration of migrants in human detention camps. About six weeks after it ended, I absolutely crashed. I was emotionally, physically, and psychologically spent. And that's when LaTosha Brown, sensing that I was struggling, reached out to me.

It was a very simple message: "Are you OK?"

I was not. I didn't want to burden her, but I explained in very short order what was happening—that I was exhausted, that a confluence of factors had come together in that moment, that I'd been completely tapped by the event and it's aftermath, and that I had work to do on myself and for others but I felt completely broken.

What she wrote to me next was revolutionary in and of itself: "Can you take some time to heal? We are in protracted struggle. We must stay healthy and focused."

I replied that I knew I needed a break but I didn't know how to take one—that I was deeply engaged in the work but also wanted to flee the public realm, that I was hurting but that I also knew I couldn't quit, and yet I couldn't keep going on this way.

LaTosha replied with this: "My people come from a long history of oppression. There were some that knew slavery would end. You have to preserve and protect your spirit; you have to believe love will win. We are uprooting years of hatred, but we will win."

She's a good friend and a wise, wise woman, that LaTosha Brown. And she offered me an invitation to breathe through revolutionary work, to pause to heal when I knew I needed it, to work to preserve and protect my spirit and to help others to do the same.

When we are engaged in the throes of revolutionary, world-changing work, we can't keep going forever on all cylinders. The work of overthrowing systemic and institutional oppression is a marathon. For some of us, it dates back centuries. And we have much to learn about the strength, the fortitude, the duration it takes to win, especially for those who have been engaged in the struggle for generations.

In yogic philosophy, there is a concept called spanda—the idea that all things, from the beating of your own heart, to your breath, to your muscles, to the nature of the universe, is one of expansion and contraction and expansion again. Sometimes, when we have been engaged in the rapid expansion of revolutionary work, putting our lives, our minds, our bodies, or our voices on the line, we must take the necessary contraction on the other side of it, or we will not be able to expand again. This duality is real. For every charge forward on the path toward change, we must take a similar pause to rest and to heal. This is how we keep going.

The work of overthrowing systems and centuries of oppression is dirty work. While we may be able to lead through it, as LaTosha does, with joy and faith, we subject ourselves to challenges along the way that are designed to break us. Oppressive structures are counting on our exhaustion. Agents of those structures are inclined to fight back and to wear us down.

Taking the rest we need, when we know we need it, is revolutionary, too. Nourishing our spirits and souls with rest, love, care, and compassion for ourselves is a way of bringing the rain to our own experience.

And then, when we rise again to greet the next cycle on the path, we are stronger, wiser, braver, and yet softer, committed to uprooting hatred, and living more fully into the space of knowing that love will win.

16.

Engaging Revolution: Co-Conspirators for Justice

Last year, I was invited to consult at a major software company. I was brought in by an Indigenous woman from South America who had been battered by the experience of working under the only white woman in senior leadership in the company. Particularly, the woman who brought me in had experienced the kinds of direct abuse from her white woman supervisor that I've described in earlier chapters, to the point of overt harm to her career trajectory. Nonetheless, in an effort to create greater gender equity in the firm, she invited me to meet with her and her boss to discuss a potential women's leadership program, which the boss had expressed an interest in implementing.

Inside that room, however, I saw firsthand the dynamic between the two women. Where my Indigenous friend suggested strategies for combating racism and sexism in the company, her white superior dismissed or diminished her points. Where my friend suggested topics for a workshop with me, her supervisor claimed senior leadership would be a "hard sell" if I didn't offer something more gender neutral. And then, as the meeting was winding down, the supervisor launched into a diatribe on how she had been so put upon in her quest to make a name for herself in the company as a woman that maybe she just needed private coaching for herself, while ignoring and dismissing the very real ways that her female staff, and particularly her Black, brown, and Indigenous staff, needed support.

I left disappointed in the outcome, knowing I would not be hired, and concerned about the power dynamic at play that minimized and divided women in the company, thanks to the supervisor's unwillingness to listen or to consider how she was operating against the interests of diverse women company-wide. Sadly, this was not the first or the last time I'd see this dynamic in operation.

۞

In the quest for real revolutionary change, we must be mindful of the ways in which systems of power work to divide us in order to keep us down. It is for this reason that I am ever wary of competition and separation between women, particularly on issues of race, and the absolute need to move beyond claimed or performative allyship by white women, and toward becoming co-conspirators for justice across racial lines.

We need to be crystal clear here that anything that works to separate and divide us keeps us from working together to create revolutionary change. It is for this reason that working on our own internalized biases and trauma is required work. When we attack one another in the language of patriarchy, vote against our own interests or for handmaidens of white supremacy or, if we're white, align with whiteness instead of women of color, we are complicit in the work of oppression. Notably, as Black activist and writer Brittany Packnett Cunningham has put it, "your whiteness will actually not save you from what the patriarchy has in store for you."*

Elizabeth Warren has described this work as follows: "You can't fix what you won't look at. . . . I screw things up, but I listen, I learn, and I fix it. That's why it's so important to move beyond being an ally and becoming an anti-racist, co-conspirator for justice. Because it's done in the hope that we really can build a better country, not just for some, but build a better country for everyone."

We must intentionally transform a key mentality that we're taught from birth, namely that when one woman wins, another one loses, and that there is only so much power, money, access, achievement to go around. We must always be unpacking our unconscious biases that strive to divide us and keep oppressive structures in power. When we do not work together, we all fail, but when we work together, we all win. Truly, when one of us succeeds, and when Black, brown, and Indigenous women in particular succeed, we all do.

To this end, being a co-conspirator for justice is in my view absolutely mandatory. So what does this look like in practice?

*Pod Save America (@podsaveamerica), "To the 53% of white women who voted for Donald Trump: your whiteness will actually not save you from what patriarchy has in store for you . . . Stop selling us out."—@MsPackyetti #PodSaveAmerica HBO, October 19, 2018, https://twitter.com/PodSaveAmerica/status/10534845016 43472896?s=20.

LEADING V. BEING LED

I am the first person to admit that I like to be in charge. I rebel against anything that is designed to limit my control over my own life, and I run from being told what to do. I have also at certain points in my life had an absolute blind faith that I could figure things out without help from anyone, and that I was usually the best person for any job that came my way.

What I have learned over time, however, is that not only does a refusal to be led make for a harder life—it also allows my privilege to thrive when others who are better suited to lead at a given moment or on a given issue are drowned out by my voice.

I have gotten much better about this over the past few years, but it has required a concerted attention to my initial impulse of privilege. A healthy dose of humility helps. A willingness to say, "I don't know what I'm doing," when it's actually true, can also lead to growth.

Most significantly, if you are a white woman, I can't state enough how much it matters right now to follow the lead of Black, brown, and Indigenous women, to amplify their work, to support them however possible (including with your wallet), and to shut up and listen. If you are engaged and surrounded by phenomenal women of color and you continue to do your own work on racism and unconscious bias, and you ask what you can do to help or support and take those requests to heart, you will start to become a true co-conspirator.

Allow yourself to be led. And remember to hold the door wherever your privilege lies.

PERFORMATIVE GESTURES V. WHAT YOU DO WHEN NO ONE'S LOOKING

Notably, your work as a co-conspirator for justice with other women must extend into places where no one is watching. It is not enough to claim to be working for revolutionary change but to not then put yourself on the line as required. It's worse yet to claim to be an ally and then refuse to live into that commitment behind closed doors. Your commitment to revolution must extend beyond making yourself look and feel good in the eyes of others, and well into putting yourself on the line for the collective good. No revolutionary change comes inside our comfort zones, and as the old saying goes, talk is cheap. Talk is also meaningless if it's not followed up by action.

While I may talk quite a bit about leveraging and undermining privilege, I also take every opportunity to call people in when I get the chance. I've had many, many instances in the last few years, for example, where I have tried to call in white men, white women, and corporate clients as a whole on their obvious gender and racial biases in hiring, promotion, and pay. I've done this in private conversations, some of which have been very uncomfortable, and in more public environments like speaking engagements or leadership trainings, and I've also done it directly to people with exorbitant amounts of access, privilege, and power when they're living in their blind spots and harming others.

In some instances, I've been attacked or dismissed out of hand. In others, though, the experience has been one of throwing a pebble into a pond, creating ripples of change. In my corporate work, when the conversations around equity are informed by those on the ground in a company who are doing work collectively behind the scenes to make a change, those conversations may be more effective coming from an outside observer like myself, and then be supported by internal work by change agents within the organization.

The most successful forms of change I've seen, though, to benefit the lives of women and marginalized people come from efforts to build alliances that have duration, and that are structured to apply pressure on multiple fronts. Consider our earlier conversation about breakthrough movements. Efforts to build alliances to create revolutionary change don't just need to happen on a nationwide or global scale. They must also happen in microcosms—in every community, organization, company, caucus, and body of government—if we are after real progress toward freedom and equity, and they must be grown for the long haul and built for duration, for as long as it takes.

You must start with yourself. It is not enough to say you want change; you must actually work for it. And that means working among and with other women and marginalized people, in secret or out loud, for the long haul. It means calling out those who continue to perpetrate harm, and calling in those who may be open to change. It means working for the betterment and freedom of everyone. You must do the work, and continue to do it, and leverage and undermine whatever privilege you have whenever you are given the opportunity. You must be forever mindful of dismantling your own internalized biases and your own privilege. And you must use your voice for change whenever you can.

A WORD ON LABOR,
EMOTIONAL OR OTHERWISE

Speaking of leveraging privilege, it's important to acknowledge that there is a big difference, for those of us who are white women, between refusing white saviorism on the one hand, and forcing Black women to do all the labor of educating others on why racist, oppressive systems need to end on the other. I've watched white executives try to force their few employees of color into doing unpaid labor on special-interest committees, not understanding that that work takes away from the work needed for those same employees to perform and advance. Similarly, I've watched men demand that female employees explain to them over and over again, with ever-increasing numbers of PowerPoints, how their policies are discriminatory, only to jettison recommendations for change for months or years, or for good.

It's of critical importance that people of privilege do not demand that those without it educate those who have it on their biases, their failings, or how to leverage or undermine the privileges they have. Do not ask those who are harmed by ignorance to take on the burden of yours. Do the work yourself and in conjunction with other invested folks who are working through the same issues.

And above all, ask how you can be of service. Ask how you can support those who are fighting for their own freedom. Ask where you are needed. Sometimes, the answer will be that you are not, in which case you must do the right thing, shut your mouth, and stay home. Sometimes, the answer will be that you are needed to put your career, your money, or your body on the line for those who can't, in which case you must do the right thing, and do that.

We rise or fall together. When one of us wins, we all do. When marginalized and oppressed people win, we all win. Divided, we lose.

LASTLY: FOR THE MEN

If you are a man who is reading this book, welcome! I'm glad you are here and that you have made it this far. I hope that you have learned much, and that you are committed to finding your inner heroine.

I need to tell you, though, that your work in holding the door is needed now more than ever. You must step aside, hold the door, and clear the way for women—and particularly Black, brown, and Indigenous women—to lead. You must be the barrier between us and those who would seek to tear us down and deny us power and impede our freedom. We need your help and we need your support.

I will remind you as well of our earlier discussion of how relinquishing privilege for the greater good feels like loss. At any moment where you find yourself thinking, "Why do I have to forego this? Why her and not me?" I'd encourage you, too, to do the work on your own unconscious biases, as well as on the fact that all of your success, your experiences, your life—whether full of suffering or full of joy—have been made exponentially easier at every step by patriarchy.

However, patriarchy has also confined you to its box. It has limited your emotional expression, your capacity to ask for support, your ability to be complete beings as well. It has brought with it shame, and constraint, and harm.

You, too, deserve to be completely human. The way to get there is to work for the equity, power, and freedom of everyone else, and to undercut your own privilege wherever you can.

The way we get to revolution is through collaboration with one another, toward the freedom of all. You, too, have a critical role to play. Co-conspiring with others requires your humility, your leverage, your kindness, and your understanding that all of us have been impacted by white supremacist patriarchy, and all of us will benefit when it ends.

For this is the thing about heroines: we don't water the earth for some but for all. The rain doesn't pour down on only a few. When we walk the path, we walk it for the collective, and the spoils we return to share benefit the totality of humankind.

17.

Engaging Revolution: Revolution for Yourself

The slogan "the personal is political" has been around for decades now, going back to the student and radical feminist movements of the sixties, and particularly radical Black feminist work propelling this topic forward.

While it's a phrase you may be aware of, in our current moment in history, I see it as a catalyst to self-examination, and one that cannot be refused.

It has never ceased to amaze me how many of us believe that our own, most intimate lives don't also count in the greater scheme of things, that somehow *we* don't also count on the path toward change.

Now is a good time to ask yourself some questions: What are

you putting up with in your own life that you wouldn't want for others? What are you allowing to remain in your life that runs counter to your beliefs and to the work you're doing in the world? How might you be putting the highest ideals you're working toward in the world on the back burner when it comes to yourself? And more broadly, what are we tolerating in our most intimate spaces that we wouldn't tolerate anywhere else, and *why*?

Truth be told, never have I had to confront this more directly than in the choice to end my own marriage.

Looking back, the last day of my marriage feels like it came quietly, though the wave I'd been riding was tidal by the time it broke in the summer of 2016. Already separated once, my husband and I had been in couples counseling for most of our marriage, largely due to his rage and my increasingly traumatized response to it. His outbursts were sudden and terrifying, for me and, later, for our children.

Throughout the photos on my phone over the eight years and then some of our marriage and separation are shots from nearly all the places we lived that include holes punched in walls, faceplates ripped from electrical sockets, broken dishwasher handles, metal garbage cans he crushed in a fit of rage in our apartment building's refuse room, a car windshield he smashed from the inside with his fist when he couldn't find a parking place, or—in the image that still shatters me—a broken baby gate that he destroyed underfoot in the middle of a fight over child care.

His violence wasn't limited to objects though. Once our first child was born, it turned in my direction. The worst of these events was not, I regret to say, the one that made me leave. It had come eighteen months earlier, when in the middle of the night, with two children under the age of two sleeping ten feet away, he slammed his hands against both sides of my head, lifted me off the ground, and shook me so hard I thought my neck might break. A 911 call followed that resulted in repeated return calls when my ex hung up the phone as I ran to hide in my daughter's room where, by then, she was crying.

In the end, I declined to have the police come to our apartment. The resignation in the voice of the female operator, the edge of disappointment and defeat that came with a sigh and a single word from her, "OK," as I rocked my child on the floor of her room with the phone at my ear, crying, is something that I will never forget for as long as I live. She wanted me to know she knew. She wanted me to know she'd heard it. She wanted me to know that she knew I was quitting, and that it probably wasn't the first time.

Why? Why did I do this? Why did I allow it to continue? Why was it not enough that night to end the marriage once and for all? These were the questions I asked myself that night, and for the next eighteen months on a daily basis.

When the end of our marriage finally came, it was on a morning where I was getting our children ready for preschool. By that point, I'd made it clear in couples counseling that if he ever put his hands on me again in anger, I was done. That morning, he was holding a cup of coffee and I was getting the kids out the door, my son in the carrier on his back, my daughter at his feet. I reached for the coffee to help him get the kids on their way, and out of nowhere he screamed, "Get your fucking hands off me," and with the full force of his six-foot-one frame, put his free hand in the middle of my chest and shoved me backward into a hall mirror.

The mirror didn't shatter, but something inside me did. What I recall in the immediate moment thereafter isn't the pain that left bruises on my back and arms, nor the shock to my body that I know I must have felt. What I remember most clearly was the expression of fear and horror on the face of my four-year-old daughter as she stood at my husband's feet in the seconds after it happened, and my son on my husband's back in the carrier, crying.

That moment was an internal revolution. Something changed, in a split second, and for good. In an absolute instant, I knew that I was finished, that this was over, and that I was unwilling, ever again, to have my children witness anything like that and think that it was normal.

It was done. I was done.

◦◦

In the weeks after that, I spent a lot of time on the phone with friends—activists, lawyers, colleagues who were experts on domestic violence. I spoke my shame, and tried to get to the root of why I had stayed for so long despite what I knew to be wrong inside my own home. My friend Robin Runge, who is a Fulbright scholar on the topic of domestic violence, said it to me best: "Domestic violence touches everyone at every level of our culture. It is a function of patriarchy. No one is immune, and it's not about you. It's about *us*."

In the years since, I have turned this over and over again in my own mind—the whys and hows of it, the depth of our own internalized bias, the necessary belief that comes with it that somehow we as women and others who have been harmed by forms of oppression aren't deserving of better, even when we consciously know the collective deserves so much more.

This is one reason why I want to make it plain to you that the revolution can't just extend to what you do outside your own home. You *must* engage in revolution for yourself, as well. We must refuse to tolerate in our own lives what we know isn't good for the collective as a whole—for otherwise, what is the point? While leaving an abusive relationship may be a prime example of this, ask yourself this as well: Are you tolerating small or large inequities for the sake of "keeping the peace" in your own home or your own life?

We must absolutely build the societal and cultural structures that allow women to leave abusive relationships, or even inequitable ones. We must absolutely value the lives of women and any marginalized person enough to create the means for us to live safely in every aspect of our lives. We must commit to this for as long as it takes. And we must also position ourselves to model a better way to our children and future generations. As often as possible, we must decline to continue allowing oppression to win the day in every part of our daily lives. We must find the courage to do it differently, to break the cultural legacies into which we were born, to revolve, to turn away, to revolt against the old ways of being. *We must fight for our own freedom as hard as we fight for the freedom of everyone else.*

But let's be clear: the choice to leave a relationship that doesn't serve you, or *any* choice to put yourself in a place of worthiness that you've never occupied before, is the *beginning*, not the end, of a revolution for yourself. Indeed, the decision to place your worthiness above the worthiness of those who don't value you is a tenuous and fragile path at first. When I left with the kids, for instance, broken and packing up our stuff, as I disassembled my kids' toddler beds and carried them down three flights of stairs in New York City alone to stuff them into the back of a Volkswagen Jetta, I would have told you that I was still in love with my husband, and I would have told you that I believed I'd failed. It was the most raw I had ever felt, and it bore the overwhelming taste of shame, because I believed it was my fault that I'd been unable to control his outbursts, stop his violence, and end his rage. Yes, I hated him for it as much as I loved him, but I hated myself even more.

Choosing revolution for yourself may come in an instant, but the work to get there takes time.

Why? Because when it comes to relationships with men, patriarchy wants women trained as caregivers and repairers. It's convenient, this complicity, that is engrained in the interpersonal and systemic oppressive structures in which we live. When men are broken and flawed, rather than leaving them to do their own work, *or recognizing that their brokenness is inherent to their power over anyone deemed less valuable*, we are supposed to take on their flaws as if they are our own, and fix them.

This isn't just true, by the way, in intimate or personal relationships. It's also true at work and in the world. I've coached countless women who have tolerated horrific abuse in the workplace and yet, when they try to leave those jobs or bosses, feel ashamed for not trying harder, fighting back, or somehow "curing" the abusive boss—often despite the fact that there's a wake of other victims that came before. I've seen the same dynamics in religious organizations, nonprofits, and wellness groups, to the same ends.

And it's also true in smaller ways: how we tolerate inequitable distribution of work in our own homes, of child care and who is expected to sacrifice for that; in the ways we are expected to tolerate microaggressions on a daily basis; in the ways in which we are assumed, still, to be responsible for the emotional labor of educating men and others of privilege when we don't have it. We more often than not just live with it, because that's what we've been taught to do.

In the face of this messaging that we are somehow responsible for the violence and failings of men and others in our lives who bear the stamp of privilege, we internalize the idea that our own value is less-than—and it's important to note that this internalization is not simple or stupid or instantaneous, but rather reinforced relentlessly in our culture and in our own families. Midway through my marriage, for instance, when things had already devolved to the point that others had witnessed my ex-husband's violence, a family member sent me a card, with what I'm sure was the best of intentions. On the face of it was the following quote: "Life isn't about waiting for the storm to pass. It's about learning how to dance in the rain." This was but one of many messages that I got throughout this time—mostly from other women, it should be said—that the most important thing was that I—*not my husband, but I*—needed to learn how to address the struggles in our marriage, his violence and abuse, be compassionate for his failings, and abide because it was my responsibility to do so.

The flip side of this is that when we finally decide that our own value should come first, that our revolution should belong to us

not just in politics and not just in policy but also in the most intimate of places and the most emotional of ways, we often end up
navigating that path alone. To this day, I still have family members who grow uncomfortable about the mention of the end of my
marriage, who will offer compassion not to me but to him. Over
and over again, I have seen this mirrored in others as well, whether
in responses to women who abandon traditional career paths to
start businesses, or opt not to have children, or come out of the
closet after years of trying to be straight, or simply decide, somewhere, somehow, that they've *had enough* of being told how, when,
or where to do anything with their lives that doesn't feel like it
works, instead of assuming the roles that the culture demands they
occupy.

So what does it mean to walk this path alone, or with minimal
support, as you try to navigate a path for yourself outside of what
you're told to be? Well, initially, I will tell you that it requires an
inordinate amount of bravery. The good news about bravery, however, is that it grows in collective. Find one person who sees you,
gets you, knows that you are capable and amazing, find one person who will tell you your value over and over again, and you will
have a launchpad. Find two or three, and you will have an army at
your back.

That army won't lessen the pain, it should be said. One of the
biggest struggles for me in all my choices to stand up for myself
first has been the abandonment of those who "should" have loved
me through them—a parent, for instance, or a sibling. That said,
this work is the place where the unpacking of culture and the
unpacking of family must come together in the work of healing.
Whether through therapy or other trauma response methodol-

ogies, body work, or spiritual process, we (and our army) must commit to transmuting our most personal pain into a force for change, and for good.

Because here's the thing: we're all entitled to joy, to happiness, to safety, to freedom. No matter who you are or where you were born, your gender identity, your orientation, the color of your skin, or the relative value society places on any aspect of your being, you were born worthy. It's the framework of oppression that teaches us otherwise, that great propaganda of hierarchy and value. On the paths we walk to becoming heroines, we must process our pain for ourselves as individuals as well as collectively, revolve away from these great lies we're told, and move toward a complete integration of our inherent value.

There is no revolution, in my view, unless we take our revolution into the quietest, most intimate spaces, and really into the very bones of who we are. At the baseline, and in the endgame of all this work, is the fact that all of us deserve to feel complete, safe, loved, valued, and happy. If we are not free to be ourselves, to live in the complete expression of our uniqueness, to own our own inherent value and to place ourselves in the world with the knowledge that we are as valuable, equally and equitably valuable, as everyone and anyone else, what are we doing? Moreover, if we do not confront the workings of oppression in our own lives, are we not condoning its continuation elsewhere?

My revolution is not just a revolution for the masses, though it is absolutely that. It is also, quite plainly, revolution for yourself.

So if you happen to find yourself, as I have on a number of occasions, in a place where you are tolerating things in your own life that you would never tolerate for your friends, your allies, your children, or your loved ones, I implore you to investigate why. If you are wracked with shame, if you can't understand how you got to where you are, if you are afraid to speak it out loud, if you are stunned at what you are living through despite what you believe to be true, you are not alone. We are taught to tolerate violence. We are taught to tolerate oppression. We are taught that it is just a part of being born as we are and not as white, straight, cisgender, able-bodied men.

The moment you recognize for yourself that you didn't bring it on, that you did not deserve it, and that it wasn't owed, the moment that you pick it all up and start over, when you carry the toddler bed down all three flights of stairs by yourself and leave with only the things you can lift with your own two arms and with two tiny children by your side, the moment you *see it as it is* and you *know that you deserve more than this* and you *walk toward that* even if you're terrified, well that, my dear and beloved one, *that moment is a revolution.*

May joy find you and walk with you all of your days. May you walk among great beings who are revolving every structure of our culture and society to give you the safety net to always choose your own worthiness over and over again. May you find hope. May you find pleasure. May you know peace. May you know freedom. May you live in the presence of joy. And may we all create it, now and forevermore, for all of us.

If we trust that we are all connected, then every act that shifts the balance of power is a revolutionary act. Every gesture that changes the status quo has a ripple effect. Every choice we make that propels us toward justice joins with all other choices collectively until what sounds like a tiny plea for freedom becomes a roar.

For in the ashes of our suffering lie the seeds of our rebirth.

And you have it within you to bring the rain, I promise you that, even if it's just in the form of your own tears until you find the pathway out.

Section Four
Rebirth

18.

Toward Liberation and New Leadership

This is the place in the journey where we get to stand in the place of transformation: holding both our vision and our conduct to account, in the place where we are informed by the past, revolving the present, and living into the future, and where we bring the rain.

None of us has ever had the benefit of living in a time where liberation and freedom for all is a reality. We have to occupy that space consciously, right now, to create it. We have to water it daily to keep it alive, constantly monitoring its growth.

One way we do that is by living in the fullness of time.

About fifteen years ago, I was lucky enough to attend a lecture on living in the fullness of time, given by Dr. Douglas Brooks, a professor of religion with a deep understanding of Hinduism based on nearly twenty years living in the household of a professor in southern India. Living in the fullness of time means that we are conscious of the fact that we are at once past, present, and future. Where you sit right now reading this sentence will be the past by the time you finish reading it. The future exists as you read the period of this sentence, because you can see the next word. If you opt to wrap your mind around it, it's obvious that we are living in the fullness of time at every moment.

Similarly, everything you have learned previously creates what's coming next. Everything in the future depends on the present and the past. We are always who we have been and who we are and who we will be, at once.

Why open a section on rebirth on such a metaphysical note? Isn't it all about action?

Well, it's critical to start any discussion of rebirth by understanding that every experience you have ever had has brought you to this point. You are, in the present, the sum of your past, and the totality of who you are creates the future. I say this because a critical part of my own healing, from the standpoint of trauma and the standpoint of revolution, has required me to integrate every horrifying experience of my life into who I am, and to transmute every single one of them into power.

And I'm going to ask you now to take a leap of faith with me: what I've written above is as true for nations as it is for every single human being.

We have an obligation to take every experience that we've had as a nation—hell, as a planet—and integrate it into who we are going forward in order to transmute our shared trauma into power.

How do we do that? We choose every day, in every action, to create new structures and new systems of equity. We choose every day, in every action, to remain vigilant of the stains of history— slavery, genocide, racism, sexism, homophobia, ableism, violence, war, even wage labor capitalism (a topic far beyond the scope of this book)—to make sure that we are constantly transmuting the trauma they've caused into real power for real people who have never had it before.

What does this mean in practice? It means that we have to birth liberation and a new model of leadership that makes every person truly free.

If we believe that we live in the fullness of time, the future is right now. If it only takes 3.5 percent of the population to birth change, then we can, at least in theory, do it instantly.

So let's think through what liberation looks like.

Imagine if all of us were free. Free to walk the streets whenever we chose. Free from state-sponsored oppression, the carceral state, and the school-to-prison pipeline. Free from xenophobia and artificial lines in the sand. Free to move and travel as we see fit. Free from violence. Free from rape. Free from harm in the form of our basic needs never being met absent labor that works us to the bone. Free to love who we love and be who we are. Free from discrimination, racism, sexism, othering. Imagine what it would mean for our children to be raised in a society without all the things we internalized and all the harm we lived through. Imagine all the possibilities pregnant in that.

It would lead to a place where each of us could live into our highest gifts. Any education you wanted to refine those gifts would be available to you. Your gifts would become an act of service to the collective. Your world would be a place of exponential cultivation. *You* would be the seed that gets planted and for whom we'd all bring the rain.

Magical, isn't it? And not impossible. Here's how.

NEW MODELS OF LEADERSHIP

So let me say first that the idea of "leadership" may feel antithetical to a world where every gift is valued. This is a good moment to acknowledge that when the only models of leadership we've seen truly valued are those that look like Machiavelli's or his female version, the notion of leadership itself is imbued with toxic qualities. Leadership acts as hierarchy, and hierarchy enforces systems of oppression.

I'm going to ask you to break out of that box of thinking.

Leadership can be something entirely different, particularly when we move into the idea that everyone in the collective has value.

Consider the idea of the seat of the teacher. In collective models of leadership, everyone has something to offer back. Thus, the person taking the seat of the teacher is the person who has something to offer. Everyone, in turn, takes the seat of the teacher for their gift. Everyone is simultaneously the teacher and the student. No one owns the seat all the time.

This is a profoundly different model from that which we're used to seeing everywhere. Hierarchies, with ever-increasing tiers and bosses, replicate or represent systems of oppression. Traditionally masculine models of leadership assume that one person knows best at each tier, and all those below them are of lesser value, and have less to contribute. It should go without saying that change can't come when only one person, or a few people, think they know it all.

Not surprisingly, I am not the first person to envision alternative models of leadership based on communal or collective value. Whole studies have been conducted around models that deconstruct traditional hierarchical leadership, including ones that have practical application *today.*

Collaborative governance, for example, which has been studied and tested by a host of scholars from Berkeley to Syracuse, is founded on the idea that systems that have functioned with power imbalances can be reformed into collaborative models. In a paper published in the *Journal of Public Administration Research and Theory* in 2008, for instance, professors Chris Ansell and Alison Gash proposed a radical re-envisioning of how historically asymmetrical (I would say structurally oppressive) leadership models could be reformed to be collaborative and inclusive.* To move toward collaborative leadership, institutions must, by design, create participatory inclusiveness, clear ground rules, and transparency. Moreover, the collaborative process itself requires trust-building; commitment to a mutual recognition of interdependence; shared ownership of the process of leadership; openness to exploring mutual gains; shared understandings of mission, common problems, and common values; pushing toward intermediate outcomes to propel forward, including small wins, strategic plans, and joint fact finding; and face-to-face dialogue that includes good faith negotiation. (I'll note here, for those of you who have been paying attention, that this sounds an awful lot like the skill set we worked to build in earlier chapters of this book.)

Rather than traditional leaders in the masculine model of dom-

---

*Chris Ansell and Allison Gash, "Collaborative Governance in Theory and Practice," *Journal of Public Administration Research and Theory* 18, no. 4 (October 2008): 543–71, https://doi.org/10.1093/jopart/mum032.

inance in leadership with which we're all familiar, Ansell and Gash suggest a facilitative model of leadership that includes empowerment of all, where the facilitator's role is to "ensure the integrity of the consensus building process itself."* This includes promoting broad and active participation by all, broad-based influence and control, and productive group dynamics.

Lastly, the facilitator role isn't occupied by just one person, but rather multiple "leaders," formally and informally, who guard the security of the process. In a later paper, Ansell and Gash described leadership in collaborative governance as follows:

> In this voluntary, shared power world, it is clear that leaders do not "command" in the same way that they might in a hierarchical organization. Leaders may bear responsibility for steering collaboratives toward efficient service delivery, consensus, or creative problem-solving, but they must work within the constraints imposed by voluntary action and shared power.†

They go on to identify three models of leadership in collaboration: steward, mediator, and catalyst, each of which maximizes unique skill sets to protect the process.‡

Now, if all of this sounds like a bunch of corporate lingo gib-

---

*Ansell and Gash, "Collaborative Governance," 594.
†Chris Ansell and Allison Gash, "Stewards, Mediators, and Catalysts: Toward a Model of Collaborative Leadership," *The Innovation Journal* 17, no. 1, article 7 (2012): 5, http://innovation.cc/scholarly-style/2012_17_1_7_ansell_gash_innovate-leadrship .pdf.
‡Ansell and Gash, "Stewards," 8.

berish, allow me to translate: what Ansell and Gash and others have proposed is a fundamental structural revolution in leadership where everyone has value and everyone has power. Every participant is invested in the decision-making process, and everyone has power over the outcome. "Leaders," rather than buck-stops-here-my-way-or-the-highway dominators, are instead stewards, mediators, catalysts for decision-making—folks who take responsibility for making the process equitable and with integrity for all, and they rotate in and out of that role with others. Most importantly, the system is always learning from itself, informing, revolving, developing as it continues.

It is a cycle. It is a path. It never stops growing. Once chosen, it continues as an evolution for all involved. At this point in the book, this may sound a little familiar.

Now, I can hear some of you already pushing back on this model of leadership in your real lives. "It's too time-intensive," might be one critique, for instance. "Not everyone knows enough to participate." "Don't we need hierarchy to be efficient?" "But we've always done it this way" could be some other arguments running through your mind, which I will just note is, once again, internalized bias justifying systems of oppression that do not serve us all.

If you are thinking these thoughts, I'd like you to consider how deeply ingrained in our synapses is the idea that there is only one way to lead. Heroines do it differently. We always have.

I have some experience with this in practicality. Though we've had some serious trials and errors in this regard, this model of collaborative governance is more or less how I have sought to run my company. We make no major decisions about what we do that are not accomplished in collaboration. I act as the facilitator most of the time—though not always, as Megan was an absolute pro at this in times of conflict. We seek input from every invested party, but not just that—we share collective responsibility for making those decisions, and the power isn't just mine alone. Indeed, there are more times than I can count when Megan in particular called me on the carpet for where I had blind spots or was missing something or simply wasn't sticking to our lived values of kindness and proactive listening, and she did it for years. She shot down ideas that made no sense and offered up new ones that I'd never have considered. She held me accountable to the process. I try to live into her spirit in this regard every day with our current team, including through shared financial outcomes.

Let's return for a moment to the idea of the temple—where we previously met our guardians who held the door. Imagine there, on the dais, a council of women and femmes and non-binary folx, key decision makers for culture and government. Every person on the council has a different set of gifts and skills. Every diversity imaginable is represented, and more than tokened, it exists in widespread representation. Everyone has an equal stake in decision-making. All voices are heard and valued. The seat of the facilitator rotates, maintaining integrity in the process. Conflict resolution, empathy, and nonviolent communication are integral to the process. Any person or group impacted by a given decision has power in the decision-making process. Those most impacted lead from the seat. Decisions are made in collective collaboration, for the greater good of all.

Now, I want to make clear that while I find this model of leadership revolutionary and rebirthing and full of hope and joy and love, it is not unrealistic. In practice, you can start living into it right now.

In any organization in which you operate, do those most impacted by a decision have power to control that decision? To take a hypercorporate example, for instance: Do those most impacted by the wages paid to frontline workers have power over the decision-making of how much they are paid? This goes beyond simply consulting with those workers; it goes toward empowering those historically without power to have as much of a vote in their future as the most titled senior executives. Moreover, can you step into the role of a facilitator, enabling conversations and decision-making about the future of your organization that lifts every voice and empowers everyone involved, despite historical power imbalances that might have precluded that?

Are you willing to abandon the power of privilege, wherever you have it, *if* you have it, that bears with it so much harm and pain to lead from a seat that could and should be occupied by all of us, so that all of us share power equally and therefore get to live fully into our best gifts?

Consider how you might apply what I'm proposing here right now. And above all, I want you to live in the fullness of possibility. Wherever you have privilege, there is room to empower those who have never had it. Wherever you have commanded a room, there is room for all of us to lead together. Wherever you have leaned into the model of dictatorial leadership, you can decide to embrace collaboration. Wherever you have been denied power or see that it has been denied to others, you can claim a different future by planting the seeds of what I'm suggesting inside your organization and your life, and tending to those seeds, watering them daily, so that they may germinate into better models for all of us.

It doesn't have to be the way we've always done it. And in fact, if we are heroines, we know already that it wasn't always done this way, and that another myth that needs to die is that collective leadership would somehow be worse than one group or one gender dominating the rest of us.

The Daughters of Danaus are a collective of women, leading together toward the watering of the future, filtering out individually and collectively what has failed, what doesn't work, and why, and allowing all that's good and worthy to flow in liberation, for the future growth of all.

A WORD ON SHARED RESOURCES, INCLUDING EMOTIONAL LABOR

I grew up in a small town in Pennsylvania, sixty miles outside of New York City, that was populated by artists and Broadway actors and hippies throughout the seventies and eighties. It's a place that was foundational to my sense of what community could look like. Jim Henson had a house less than a mile from mine that he would wrap in a massive red bow at Christmastime. The Bucks County Playhouse welcomed stars from Broadway productions in small shows that packed the house. Gay clubs like The Cartwheel and the New Prelude were full to the brim every Friday and Saturday night. It was diverse, creative, populated by communes, hippies, young families, farms, and a thriving gay community.

I grew up surrounded by gay men who would not survive the

eighties. AIDS decimated our local community, and I saw first-hand, and not for the last time, how massive government neglect could kill people on an enormous scale, but also what collective activism in a community could mean to our common survival. I saw my father, a white, straight cisgender male, convince others in our community why an AIDS hospice was needed, and speak out against fear. I saw gay doctors in my community counterbalance fear of infection with kindness and caregiving. I saw us bury our own with love, and teach safe-sex workshops to protect survivors.

Throughout my childhood and teenage years in that small Pennsylvania town, there was a regular event that marked the turning of the seasons, and that grew in significance for me the older I got: the migration of the Canadian geese. Our town was a stop along the path of that migration from the North to the South. For a few weeks every spring and fall, the honking of the geese overhead marked the turning of another year.

You couldn't grow up in that town and not know a lot about geese. I can't remember how I learned so much of what I know about them, as it bled into our experiences every single year of my childhood. I can tell you off the cuff that the V formation in which geese fly is designed to cut the headwinds as they are flying. The V itself reduces wind drag for every goose, no matter where they are positioned along it. Moreover, as each goose flaps its wings, it creates an updraft on which all those behind are buoyed. By flying in this formation, they extend the distance they can fly by an enormous margin—something like 70 percent.

Notably, each goose takes turns at the point of the V, so that when one is exhausted, another takes the turn to lead. Their honking, moreover, is designed to encourage those in front of them to keep going. And if a goose falls out of formation? Two other geese stop to stay with the fallen goose, offering protection and companionship until the fallen goose is well enough to continue, or passes on.

I have considered this formation a metaphor for leadership in community, and how it was practiced within my own, for a long time. It turns out that I am not the first to do so. As Dr. Harry Clark Noyes observed in 1992:

> People who share a common direction and sense of community can get where they are going more quickly and easily because they are traveling on the thrust of one another. When a goose falls out of formation, it suddenly feels the drag and resistance of trying to go it alone and quickly gets back into formation to take advantage of the lifting power of the bird in front. If we have as much sense as a goose, we will stay in formation with those who are headed the same way we are.*

In my adult life, over time, geese became a metaphor for leading in community, in the flow of nature and the seasons, and in the expansion and contraction of individual effort. As we strive to create new models for leading together in breakthrough ways, we must be mindful that we rise or fall together. Across every marginalized group and in every community, we must take turns leading, we must sometimes be the one to cut the path, we experience the benefit of those who cut the headwinds, we lift up those coming

---

*Harry Clark Noyes, "The Goose Story," *ARCS NEWS* 7, no. 1 (January 1992).

behind us, and we take encouragement from their voices to carry us on.

Now is a time that I have to remind you that Black, brown, and Indigenous women, and people of color in general, have been cutting the headwinds of change alone for far too long. The expression "Follow Black women" is not a mandate to exploit their labor, emotional or otherwise, which I hope any white person reading this book would recognize by this point as a replication of structures of oppression. Rather, to me, following Black women means *centering* on the experiences of Black women (and other people of color); listening to Black women as leaders; following their leadership; and internalizing those lessons as we build a better future.

This means that white women must adopt the point of the V in calling in our own and educating ourselves to cut the headwinds of racism that have exhausted Black women for so long. We must ask how we can do better, be better allies, uplift and center more effectively, *and then we must act* in collaboration and in support. This starts with educating ourselves, including by reading the works of the authors mentioned in earlier chapters, joining organizations that work to undermine white supremacist patriarchy wherever it lives, and asking how we can best be of service and be better allies.

Birth is a process, and it is exhausting. Rebirth requires us to not demand more of those who have already given so much when we all have the capacity to dismantle privilege and the systems that condone and further it. The more that we do that work, the faster will be the process that leads to all of us benefiting from the uplift, to all of us sharing power and work, to all of us caring for those who need it most, and to all of us traveling exponentially farther on the shared wings of one another. In the process, all that distraction of racism and sexism and other forms of oppression, all that malignant impact that pulls us away from the real work, will end, and we'll be able, together, to focus on what really matters: freedom, equity, liberation.

Together, on the winds of change, we rise.

VIGILANCE IN REVOLUTION AND REBIRTH

Now, I must remind you of one small fact about the Daughters of Danaus: their work is never-ending. For all time, they are filters, waterers, rainmakers, and that work never stops. So, too, is the work for all of us who care about liberation and rebirth.

We must be constantly vigilant of our own internalized biases, of the stain of centuries of barbarism, violence, and inequity, and how it lives in us. *This work will never end*, and that's a good thing. It is not a burden, but an honor, to be alive at a time where we are gifted with the chance to change *everything*. We must not blow that opportunity by letting our guard down on the constant work that needs to be done to repair that from whence we came.

At every bend in the road, our self-examination and the examination of our actions in relation to others must be constant. This is particularly true in any organization that needs cultural or institutional revision. We must always be on the lookout for falling back on old ways of doing things and old ways of thinking and being that cause harm. Our revolution must be relentless, because oppression has been relentless for far too long.

I will remind you again here that perfectionism is a tool of oppression, and we can all expect, somewhere along the line, to fuck up. That's OK. Be accountable to your blind spots and to others'. Listen and learn and commit to doing better. Every one of us is steeped in inequity from birth, and we must strengthen ourselves daily against it as we unlearn it.

You can do this. *We* can do this. We are here because we are on the path of the heroine. We can do hard things. We are *so lucky* to be alive to do hard things. And if we do them together, for as long as we're here, those coming after us may find it so much easier to be here than we have.

19.

Toward Joy

E ndemic to liberation is *joy*. This, by the way, is another lesson I've learned so clearly from LaTosha Brown. In her work as a cofounder of Black Voters Matter, I've watched her mobilize young men who thought their votes didn't count, elders who'd been prevented from accessing the polls, and whole towns of folks who have felt abandoned into action and change.

Her most powerful tool in this process? Joy. LaTosha dances and sings through organizing, celebrates Black power and liberation, feeds and nourishes all those she encounters, and creates revolution with the brightest smile imaginable. I adore her for it. She has taught me so much.

And if joy is endemic to liberation, I need to remind you of something else: you can't experience joy in rebirth if you can't feel anything at all. One of the effects of surviving centuries of systemic oppression is that most of us who have been subject to it in one form or another have developed quite serious coping mechanisms for numbing the pain.

Personally, I decided to stop drinking in the middle of 2020, five months into lockdown, in part because I was tired of feeling so little other than rage. I did not bottom out, I did not identify as an alcoholic (and still don't), and while I was certainly drinking a lot, I wasn't drinking to the point where I couldn't function in any aspect of my life. I didn't join AA, though I did join a sobriety group online, filled with amazing people from around the globe who found the model of AA, created by two white men in the 1930s who were hardcore Christians, unwelcoming but still wanted accountability.

I quit because I simply began to scare myself with how fast I was to anger, how little I felt *anything else,* and how infrequently I was able to identify, in any way, shape, or form, what might bring me joy.

In the months since then, as I've explored for the first time in my adult life what it means to live fully present, all the time, to all of life's struggles and celebrations, I've considered quite a bit how all that which has been marketed to numb us—smoking, alcohol, shopping, celebrity, social media, all of it—has been designed to distract us not just from the possibility of creating a better world, but also from revolutionary joy. The better we feel, the more we experience the totality of our humanity and the easier it is for us to find common ground across intersectional landscapes. Joy *is* revolutionary.

Our collective rebirth must include watering ourselves with hope and laughter and real, honest to goodness joy. If you haven't felt it for a while, you must seek it out. Right now, write down three things that you know bring you joy, and go do them (safely, of course, and with all due regard for other human beings). For me, at the moment that I am writing this, those three things include dance parties with my kids, playing with our pandemic puppy, and getting lost in a great book.

There are no peaks without valleys, no sunshine without rain, and you must be willing to ride the current of your life in all its magnificent cycles and lessons to integrate the reasons why you are here. Collectively, we must commit to being present, perhaps more so now than ever before, to the changes we need to make. Opportunities like the ones we are living through right now don't come often, and the groundswell of need and awareness demands our conscious presence to the work that is required.

Examine what you are numbing. Look at it. Ask yourself if your choices are grounded in awareness or instead in coping mechanisms that no longer serve you.

Prepare for all the good that can come by choosing to feel it all. Joy is liberation, and this revolution is calling your name.

A WORD ON EMBODIMENT AND ITS REWARDS

At certain times in my life, I've worked so hard that I've forgotten to eat, drink any water, or get up and walk around for hours at a time. The consequences of this are serious, for when we are not in touch with our bodies, we are not in touch with our intuition, our gifts, or our complete selves. Particularly in the final weeks leading up to the 2020 election, on which I worked nonstop for four years and roughly twenty hours a day for the final twelve weeks, I struggled to stay connected to myself. I knew that if I didn't keep up regular practices, I'd suffer in the long run, and so I carved out time every day for exercise and meditation. I also worked hard to make time to go for a walk with my kids, and to monitor my breathing.

The good news is that once the election was called, I was present enough to recognize that relief and hope were coming in waves. Fear was still present, too, as was anger, and the height of the COVID pandemic wasn't yet upon us even as vaccines began to roll out of warehouses in Michigan. But by early December, I sat down to map out my work for 2021, and sensations that I could not name began to flood into me.

They started as a sense of being able to breathe again, as though immediate terror were abating and my central nervous system could stop firing on fight or flight all the time. My physical body began to get grounded, my breath eased. Then, gradually, in dreams, things began to open up in strange and interesting ways. Rather than having night terrors about being stalked by Trump goons, I was dreaming about friends, ex-lovers, allies in the fight, and we were laughing, smiling, pushing toward better things. I righted wrongs in past relationships, created worlds of service and vision, spent dinners with modern-day witches and magic-makers, all in the dreamscape. It was a fascinating departure from the immediate hell we'd all been living in for nearly five years at that point, and from all the traumas resulting from that.

One night, about three weeks after the election, I found myself preparing to go to bed, when a video came across my Twitter feed with a lot of performative outrage and discomfort in the attached commentary. A woman, a bodyworker with a focus on female empowerment, was dancing with her partner. It was slow and sensual, supported and beautiful, but her comments about "feminine flow" were drawing scorn. I paused. I watched it again. It felt familiar. I saw in the discomfort of the comments a discomfort with this version of femininity, with the shadow and the light of it, and most significantly with her *freedom* in the presence of her partner. I paused again.

And then I vanished for a moment into the past, back to 2003 to a certain partner, a man who was so connected to himself and to me that it was the first time in my life where I could completely surrender to the experience of sex. I'm not a big God person in the traditional sense, but this was the closest I've ever gotten to something I'd consider to be divine. I'd never trusted anyone in bed the way I trusted him, and the experience of fucking him is still, almost twenty years later, as perfect in memory as it was in practice. He was breathtaking in his embodiment and in his focus on the mutuality of it, just absolutely committed to making it as rich an experience for both of us as humanly possible. I'd never felt so safe with another human being as I did with him. We were connected, sensual even with our clothes on, in the flow of everything together, protected, and above all, knew that together, we were well worth the taking of time. It was the kind of love and sex together that wakes you up on every level and reminds you of why you are here.

It took me three years to get over him when it ended, but the start of it? Whew. Those were a good six months. I was free, I was open, I was completely myself, I was with someone who met me exactly where I was, and I was really fucking happy.

And now here I was, in the waning days of the Trump era,

lying in bed watching a video on Twitter, my kids asleep down the hall and the dogs asleep by my feet. What was this, this thinking about moments and conversations and bodies I hadn't thought about in forever? What was this thing I was returning to and re-birthing and bringing forward from the past into the present and maybe the future? What was it?

A smile crept across my face. Oh. That.

Desire. Longing. Joy. Anticipation. The completeness of our humanity. Welcome back, it said, to life.

This is your reminder that your embodiment is a part of the reason why you are here. One of my long-time yoga philosophy teachers talks about how the whole point of embodiment is desire—that the divine wants to play in and through us, and that desire is its expression. We were born of desire, we create through desire, we rebirth ourselves, over and over, through the desire for something better, more meaningful, more just, more free.

Desire is what drives us on to rebirth in all things. We long for a better world. We long for connection with others and with the land we live on. We long for freedom to live and love in highest alignment with who we are. We long to build a future that works for all of us. We *want that*. And we get to choose it, or not, with every breath we take.

Not all that long ago, I saw that man again. I was invited to a family celebration with my kids, shortly after I was divorced, and we ended up sitting not far from each other, chatting like old friends as my little ones ran circles around the room. At the end of the event, we walked outside together, and he turned to me, embraced me, and then looked at my children, and back at me. "Elizabeth," he said, with not a small amount of affection, "you've done good." It said so much while saying just enough, because he was right, and he knew, and he saw it, over years and distance and a lot of love. All that had existed between us was still there, living in the present, and guiding toward the future.

What is past is present and what is present births the future. When you live into what you desire the most for yourself and for the world, and you're in alignment with the best of who you can be, you create hope, purpose, freedom, and joy in every step you take.

20.

Toward the Future

Part of the magic of being human is that we don't always know what's coming next. When I stood on my patio as Megan was dying, I didn't know for sure if I could bring the rain, and yet, suddenly, there it was. Every time we set out on a new cycle of the heroine's journey, we don't know where we're going to end up, but we must trust our intuition, walk forward on faith, and above all, keep going.

As I sit here writing the final words of this book in December 2020, I don't know where the path might have led us by the time you are reading this. What is past is present now, and will be carried forward into the future where you sit as you read this. Perhaps your present is already better than the one I'm sitting in. Today, as I type this, the very first dose of the COVID vaccine has been administered inside the United States. Chances are good it's a much safer present that you are sitting in now. The fullness of time in which I sit certainly hopes so.

On the circle of the compass, much like the circle of the heroine's journey, True North is the place of unknowing. It is where we start the journey—the place where we know that we are being called but we do not know toward what—and it is the place to which we return at the journey's end, with the spoils of our stories and the lessons learned and for a moment of peace and calm, before the cycle begins again and the journey calls us on.

While we sit here propelling forward into the future, so much is happening in our wake. Our children are growing up so fast. Generations of heroines coming up behind us are counting on those of us at the front of the V to create change so that their task will be lighter, their gifts more fruitful, their work more rewarding, their world more equitable and free. They are cheering us forward with song. They are watching us, at every step, move closer to the future we want to build. We who are heroines are bridge-walkers from the present to the future, and all those future generations need us to be the light that guides the way through the darkness of this time.

We have lived through extraordinary, heartbreaking things, every one of us. Each generation of heroines that came before us has as well. We stand on the shoulders of giants, and we light the path for those who are coming next.

Here, in this moment, we sit in a portal: Will we change at light speed now that we have the chance? Will we release what doesn't serve, heal the wounds at the foundation of our nation, break through to a future we can't yet see? Will we choose to truly become heroines for all time?

I hope so. For the first time in my lifetime, I believe we stand a real chance.

We must keep going, ever recognizing and reconciling with our history, revolving all that cannot stand, rebirthing ourselves and our world over and over again into a better future.

The work is hard. The path is lifelong. But there is joy and community and hope, and the spoils of hard-won lessons, and all the blessings of being sisters on the journey, arm in arm.

I believe in us, my sisters, we, the bearers of the water, we, the daughters who survived it all to bring the rain.

We were here to bear witness as it all went up in flames, we are here to dance in the cremation ground, and we are here to wield the waters of our rebirth.

All that power lies within us.

For the sake of the future that is counting on every single one of us becoming heroines: claim it.

EPILOGUE

Seven days after the 2016 election, exhausted and spent and already plotting a path toward what it would take to survive and resist through the coming four-plus years, and with little idea of what the future might bring, I crawled into bed in my apartment in Brooklyn. I knew that a new leg of my own journey, and our collective journey, had only just begun. I had no idea what the future would bring, but I knew that the path was calling and we were on our way.

That night, I had a dream that could best be described as a vision. When I woke the following morning, a force to write it down blew through me like the elements, and it would not be denied. This is what emerged.

Elizabeth Cronise McLaughlin updated her status.

November 17, 2016 · 👥 ▾

Deep in the dreamworld last night, I was in an enormous field with other women-- some were strangers, others were sisters I have walked with in this life, some old friends like Sianna Sherman, Laura Tulumbas Juell, Becky Rygg, others newer compatriots like Julianne Hausler, Vanessa Couto, Lindsay Pera, Claire Hayes, Tereska Haman James, Molly Knight Forde . . . so many of us, known and unknown to me.

And in the field, we were in the midst of initiation.

From the late night, into the dawn, we initiated eachother. We danced around each woman one by one as families and friends sat on the sidelines looking on. We held hands, and blessed eachother, and cleansed eachother with tears and laughter, we put our hands on eachother, and held on when we needed to.

We each stepped into the circle, and circles upon circles, throughout the night in this field, one by one, woman by woman, thousands of us.

And though the rain rose, and the wind howled, and the trees around us shed their leaves and the skies opened up and the lightning came, and the onlookers thought we would not make it, we kept going. We were not afraid.

And when it was my turn, I stepped into the circle and felt the hands and arms and force of thousands of women around me. I was held and I was loved and I was danced and I was witnessed. The night got darker and I closed my eyes and just allowed myself to be held and seen and touched. And when I opened my eyes, the sun was rising.

And as the sun came up full force, we were together in that field as sisters-- all of us-- thousands of us-- with flowers in our hair and laughter and celebration and joy, and we saw eachother as if we were seeing eachother for the first time, as we had always been, and we were happy. Powerful, connected, aligned, untouchable, and as fearless as the earth, as nature, as the circles of time, and we honored one another.

And then I woke up.

So let me say this to you this morning, my sisters: I will stand with you through the storm, and I will witness your struggle, and I will hold you when you need it, and I will honor your strength when you don't.

And though the storms may rage and the sky may open up and the world may appear to be ending, I will keep going.

Because on the other side of where we are now may very well be freedom. And I am not afraid of the darkness. I am more powerful than it will ever be. So are you.

Love to all this morning. Love to all.

~E

In all that you do, in every step you take on the path of your heroine's journey, set fire to that which no longer serves, get grounded in the earth and the ashes and plant the seeds of possibility, be buoyed by the winds of change, and above all, bring the rain.

Because on the other side of where we are now may very well be freedom. We are not there yet, but we are walking the path to it together.

And I am not afraid of the darkness. I am more powerful than it will ever be.

And so, my friend, are you.

ACKNOWLEDGMENTS

First and foremost, I must thank my extraordinary agent, Wendy Sherman. You chased me for a book proposal for two years, and were convinced that I had something to offer that was desperately needed at this moment in history even when I doubted it. You have been an amazing advocate and a great friend.

My editor, Leah Trouwborst, has shown such patience and kindness to me throughout this process, offering critical feedback, a wise eye, and a quiet fortitude through the time it took to write this. Thank you for your faith. Thank you also to Adrian Zackheim, who believed in this book from the start, and to the entire team at Portfolio for your work in bringing it to life.

As well, my publicist Kathleen Carter has brought her special magic to this process for all of us, and Sarah C. B. Guthrie contributed her artwork for the cover. Thanks to you both.

Carole DeSanti was a sister on the path, a collaborator on high-level concepts, and a catalyst to the process of transformation that led to the end product of this book. I will always be grateful for our conversations along the way.

My father, Ron Cronise, has long believed that at heart I am a writer. Thank you for always being my champion, for your endless curiosity and lifelong commitment to learning, for breaking the chains of legacies, and for showing our family the meaning of unconditional love. Thank you also to my beloved stepmother, Judy Cronise, who is the absolute heroine of our family and the guardian of my children's beautiful hearts and minds; you saved us, and built a new family from the ground up. Thank you also to my sisters and brother for putting up with me. I love you all so much, no matter what, always and forever.

My outlaws, Sharron Coleman and John Vitek, are my behind-the-scenes cheer squad who also detail my car, mind the garden, and feed the kids popcorn in bed when I'm on the road in non-pandemic times. I can't believe my luck in getting custody of you in the divorce.

Within the circles in which I travel, there are many extraordinary heroines who have changed my life, sometimes in an instant, and who have taught me so much. They include but are not limited to, in no particular order, Claire Hayes, Kris Goodfellow, Vanessa Couto, Midwin Charles, Samantha Brody, Deni Luna, Keisha Shields, Lindsey Pera, Sarah Love, Donna Helete, Celia Ward-Wallace, Brenda Villa, Sianna Sherman, Susanna Harwood Rubin, Kimberly Kyle Hall, Susan Knape, Rosie O'Donnell, Susana Crespo, Karen Lautanen, Elsie Escobar, Cindy Gallop, Charlotte Clymer, Melanie Campbell, Avis DeWeever, Robin Runge, Collette Flanagan, Mutale Nkonde, Tara McMullin, Tricia Nelson, Cathy Harris, Heather McCabe, Kira Hudson Banks, Rikke Brogaard, Tracy Silver, Tolu Olubumni, Eliza Orlins, Amy Lesko, Samantha Ronson, Maya Wiley, Marsha Levy-Warren, Rachel McDavid, Alyssa Milano, Amy Miller, Kaji Dousa, Debra Messing, Sarah Kendzior, Heather Cox Richardson, Jessica Pennington, Melissa Smith Conway, Denise Duffield-Thomas, Abby Tucker, Pam Keith, and Selina Davis, who have all contributed their spirit, their work, their support, and their friendship at critical moments along the path. Thank you.

Joanna Pena-Bickley, Kat Gordon, Bethany Williamson, Melanie Majerus, Heather Odendaal, and a number of other women who are subject to NDAs have been fearless in uplifting my work in the world, including at places like Amazon, Google, and PwC. Thank you for your support.

To Toby Gialluca and Claiborne Yarborough: I feel like we are fire-walkers. Thank you for your will, your patience, your creativity, your commitment, and for continuing to walk the talk. As well, Toby helped me sort out some really tough stuff in the final edits of this book; thank you for letting me be vulnerable.

Tanya Selvaratnam told my story as she told her own. The clarity that came with seeing my story printed anonymously in the *New York Times* as a part of your piece on domestic violence was a profound, shocking, indelible gift. Thank you for all your bravery, and for telling me at a critical turning point that it was mandatory that I stop playing small and start walking with people at the top of their game. That conversation made all the difference, to everything.

Amanda Steinberg: girl, look at us.

Connie Vasquez is my friend, my colleague, and my ally, and

gave me a chance to tell my story as a survivor at the #MeToo RallyNYC in December 2017. Ride or die, lady. I am so proud to call you my friend.

Melody Biringer and Cordila Jochim walked with me through a torturous summer in Seattle, and Ana Scolari and Anastasia Walker have been dear friends in daily life in Southern California. Thank you.

LaTosha Brown, you taught me the meaning of joy in revolution and encouraged me to remember to heal. You have modeled a better leadership for all of us and your spirit is foundational to this book. I am so grateful for you.

Mary Trump and I share a pub date. You have inspired me and I am so grateful that you chose to walk the path of the heroine. Joy Reid and Glennon Doyle, thank you for your kindness and generosity and encouragement at moments where you could have said nothing. It really, really mattered, and I am so grateful for your grace.

To Sara Bareilles, for the music that carried me all the way through this book, I bow to you and your weathermaker heart.

Tereska James, Jamie Leonhart, Julianne Hausler, Laura Tulumbas, Julie Anna Potts, Audrey Berland, Michelle Ross Daniels, and Elizabeth Meadows: you are my soul sisters in life, across many miles and many years and many lifetimes, and I would not be here without you. You are my support in times of trouble and resounding sources of celebration in times of joy. You forgive me, love me, tell it to me straight, remind me that I can't fix everything (at least not all at once), and you show up, always, no matter what. You let me be real and complete even when it feels like there is nowhere else I can be that. I love you so much.

To the men who have been friends and allies over many years to whom I can always turn for support and reminders of who I am: Douglas Brooks, Dave Stine, Greg Collett, Alex Barnett, Noah Maze, Kevin Hoover, Micah Meryman, David Gross, Jeff Ragovin, Christo Braun, Steven Popper, and Jamie Bernard, thank you for seeing me. Thank you also to Elie Mystal, for always making me laugh while rigorously backchecking my legal analysis on Twitter; to Fred Guttenberg, for your courage and for modeling the transformative power of grief in action; to Joaquin Castro, for your relentless commitment to justice even when no one is looking; to Eric Swalwell, for the encouraging clarity of your leadership; and to Malcolm Kenyatta, for the depth and the brightness of the path you walk toward a better future for all of us.

To Brittany Zeman, Chelle Weech, Zsofi Koller, Brandi Bernoskie, Vanessa Couto, and the entire extended team at the Gaia Project for Women's Leadership over the past ten years, none of this would be possible without you. To Brittany especially, thank you for walking with me through the Valley of the Shadow of Death. There are few who understand as well as we do what we lost when we lost her.

To the #ResistanceLive audience, thank you for helping me to keep the faith at the darkest moments and for reminding me to always propel toward hope, as I hope I have also done for you. To all those who have inspired, challenged, and changed me along the way, thank you. To the RISE OGs: yes, you, too, especially.

To Deborah Gibbon and Megan Baker and all the ancestors with their eyes on me: I stand on the shoulders of giants, and I hope I am doing your spirits justice.

And lastly to my daughter and my son, who are the reason, the purpose, and the meaning of it all: I love you to the sun and the moon and the stars and the earth and back again, forever and ever. Thank you for choosing me to be your mama. You are the most wonderful human beings I know, and it is the highest honor of my life to share this messy, loud, and beautiful existence with you. We are peacemakers and bridge-walkers and superheroes, my loves, and we are in it together, for all time.

INDEX